TABLE OF CONTENTS

CHAPTER 1
a community stirs — 1

CHAPTER 2
Kingston Road — 29

CHAPTER 3
horses and hot tips — 47

CHAPTER 4
the Lion's share — 61

CHAPTER 5
love that Leuty! — 79

CHAPTER 6
music man, muscular males, and clean water — 89

CHAPTER 7
Queen Street — 103

epilogue — 117

bibliography — 121

acknowledgements

Ken Bingham, Sheila Blinoff, Andy Buhot, Beaches Lions Club, Lou Cauz, Lido Chilelli, Paul Christie, David Crichton, Geoffrey Dashwood, Lynn Gatherall, Donnie Harris, Betty Isbister, Frank Jacques, Myrt Lamb, Larry Milbury, Graeme Moore, Jim Mossman, Brian Prideaux, Ted Randall, Doreen Sharland, Don Snider, Len Stanley, Carole Stimmell, John Walsh, and Bill Wheeler.

special thanks to

The Beach Metro Community News, The Toronto Archives, Barbara Weissman and Maureen McPhee of the Beaches Library for help with the library's invaluable local history collection, Gene Domagala, Beach historian and activist, and John Rygh, photographer.

To judymarthadave

the Beaches route

Editor World: It is probable that many of our citizens may consider the question of the eastern entrance of railways in the city merely one affecting the residents of that particular locality, but I desire to draw the attention of your readers to some of the facts in connection with the case, which show that every citizen has a direct personal interest in this matter.

The Beach at the eastern end of the city is now the only one left by the railways, and the bathing and boating facilities there are enjoyed by many thousands. A lake shore line as proposed by the Grand Trunk would entirely ruin over two miles of waterfront, while passing through no less than four parks, the only ones near Toronto on the lake shore.

Letter to the Editor
Toronto World March 2, 1907

CHAPTER 1

a community stirs

In 1900 tenting was an inexpensive way to spend a summer at the Beach. The young man at the left reading the Sunday World, the Telegram's Sunday paper, is George "Jimmy" Lamb.

The first day of 1900 dawned clear and cold in Toronto. The overnight temperature had dropped to minus 13 degrees Celsius. While the daytime temperature reached a relatively mild minus seven degrees, moderately strong, southwesterly winds made it seem colder. Despite the slight improvement in the weather, the general mood in the city was sombre, as indeed it was throughout the young nation. The front page of the January 1 edition of the *Globe*, 12 pages, two cents, was dominated by news of the Boer War—and the news was not good.

A group of young, single gentlemen enjoy an outing by the waterfront.

A force led by Colonel Baden-Powell had been repulsed while attacking a fort near Mafeking with 100 killed or wounded. The embattled British garrison involved in the Siege of Ladysmith had issued a desperate cry for reinforcements. A volunteer Canadian contingent of 1,061 officers and men, including four nurses and four reporters, had arrived in Africa on November 23 aboard the steamship *Sardinia*, but it would be a while before they could make their presence felt. The young Canadians fought in several major battles. By the end of the war in 1902, an estimated 242 Canadians had died in the fighting.

In 1901 Queen Victoria's death signalled the end of an era, but even as the British mourned her passing, a new day was beginning to dawn in that part of Toronto now known as the Beaches or the Beach. What to call the area has been a matter of contention for many years. The subject will come up again later in this book, just as it does to this day on a regular and often heated basis whenever two or more area residents gather.

In 1900 the *Toronto World* newspaper reported that 287 houses and 91 tents were located east of Woodbine Avenue near the lakefront. Gradually the area was growing from its sparsely populated beginnings. People were starting to regard it as more than just a place to spend the summer months. By 1906 the *Toronto Star* reported that about 250 families lived there year round. The Toronto Street

A postcard of the beachfront with the Balmy Beach Club in the background.

BEACH AVENUE VIEW, EAST TORONTO, ONT.

A toboggan outing along Queen Street East. Ross's Drugstore on the left is now Quigley's restaurant and bar. Note the spelling of Beech Avenue.

Railway, forerunner to the Toronto Transit Commission, gradually extended its tracks down to what is now the Neville Park loop, and the amusement parks that were established at different times along the beachfront helped popularize the district. Finally East Toronto was annexed by the city. Over the next few years local improvements—such as paved streets, better police and fire protection, and a good sewage system— began to be implemented.

Alice Keys was seven years old in 1902 when she moved with her family from Sherbourne Street to a house on Spruce Avenue, now Spruce Hill. In her memoirs she wrote, "There was no loose talk of the Beaches back then, there was Kew Beach, centred on Lee Avenue, and just to the east lay Balmy Beach, pronounced Bahmy by the purists, and Bammy by the rest of us."

She recalled that the surroundings around her new home were distinctly rural in character. The dense woods were carpeted with flowers such as lily of the valley, jack-in-the-pulpit, red tiger lilies, and trilliums, all of them growing among tall trees that were ideal for climbing and also for naming streets. Silverbirch, Balsam, Pine, and Beech all threw their friendly shade on the youngsters playing in their midst. Pine trees were also considered by children to be good for climbing, but this attitude was not shared by their mothers. The sticky residue took hours of scrubbing and pails of lard to clean off garments and the operation usually concluded with a good scolding and an increase in the number of chores to be done by the tree climber.

A COMMUNITY STIRS

An early game of shinny on the pond at what is now Glen Stewart Park.

When winter came, children and adults tobogganed down the long hills stretching south from Pine Street or skated on the ice in Small's Pond, so in many ways the sleepy little neighbourhood was a natural playground. There were disadvantages, however.

Trips to the water pump were a necessity in the Beach in the early 1900s. This pump was located in the front yard of a home on Herbert Street.

Alice Key's family home on Spruce Avenue was only the third house on the street. The street itself was just a sandy path leading uphill from Queen Street through dense bush north of Pine Street to Kingston Road. Among the few houses scattered along the route were several large family tents with curtained bedrooms, usually connected by an open platform to a small kitchen tent. Household water was carried from a pump at Beech Avenue and Pine, and gas for the stove and lights came in by pipelines that often froze in cold weather.

Indoor plumbing and sewers were still a few years into the future. House fires were commonplace. A volunteer fire department served the area without a great deal of help from residents—unless, of course, it was their house that was ablaze. Getting water to the scene quickly was always a problem, especially if the nearest well was a few blocks away, so the first resident to show up with a pail of water was given 50 cents for his efforts.

There was no door-to-door postal delivery in those days either. Mail was picked up at Ross's drugstore on the northwest corner of Beech and Queen. It was a long structure with a big, round stove that every day attracted a collection of old-timers who swapped gossip and filled the air with tobacco smoke, while jostling for choice locations near the stove's welcoming heat.

The store also had a soda fountain that was manned by the owner's three sons, Jack, Austin, and Hector. When asked what flavour you wanted, it was considered quite witty to reply, "Oh Hector, give me nectar." This phrase was repeated day after day, always to the accompaniment of uproarious laughter. While it is not known what effect this had on poor Hector over the years, it could not have been a good one.

Eaton's and Simpsons delivered goods from their downtown Toronto stores and the wagons were pulled by gleaming, brown horses from Eaton's or hand-

This modestly clad trio poses prettily in Lake Ontario circa 1920.

A hardworking young man performs a family chore on the front yard of his home on Scarborough Road.

some greys from Simpsons. A lot has changed from those days, of course, but one activity remains the same, and that is refreshing dips in Lake Ontario. Then as now, even the bravest could not stay in the cold waters very long, and dressing for the swim probably took more time than the swim itself. Women

WINTER AT MUNRO PARK, TORONTO.

The grounds at Munro Park were deserted on a cold winter day.

wore sailor blouses with voluminous bloomers attached over long skirts and stockings. Men bundled up in two-piece cotton swimsuits, long-sleeved jerseys, and knee-length pants. Fortunately there were other diversions that did not require such elaborate preparations.

Victoria Park, the first of the amusement parks that drew summer visitors to the area, was on the site of the R. C. Harris Filtration Plant. It boasted a circular canal around which models of Christopher Columbus's fleet of *Nina*, *Pinta*, and *Santa Maria* sailed in endless circles, but the main attraction was the Donkey Ride, where the docile animals trudged around an enclosure carrying excited youngsters on their backs.

When the park closed in 1906 after operating for 28 years, the donkeys were

A COMMUNITY STIRS 9

A human pyramid takes shape on Scarborough Beach. The two gents on either side at the rear could not have been comfortable in their hats, suits, and ties on a warm summer day.

Two elaborately coiffed young ladies pose in front of the amusement park tower.

turned loose on their own to graze in nearby fields and eventually they simply disappeared from the scene. A fruitless attempt was made to charge the owners but that casual cruelty was typical of the indifferent treatment accorded many animals in those times.

The closing of Victoria Park did not mean the end of popular entertainment in the area because immediately to the west a facility called Munro Park had been operating successfully since 1896. It featured eye-popping attractions such as a 150-foot Ferris wheel, a dance pavilion, seating for 5,000, and daily performances provided by the finest troupes from Britain and the United States.

The attractions far overshadowed the fare provided at Victoria Park in its prime, but the two venues did share one aspect in common. In the interests of law and good order, the granting of liquor licences was firmly opposed by the park owners. While this undoubtedly appeased those who frowned on drinking, it may very well have done wonders for the sale of hip flasks. These items held several ounces of spirits and were usually about eight inches high with straight sides. The deluxe models had one curved side that fit snugly in the back pocket of one's trousers, thus hindering detection by the law officers who patrolled the parks.

So propriety ruled on the park grounds themselves, but when the lights went out and the crowds went home a different behaviour pattern would emerge in nearby rooming houses rented out to the entertainers. A number of actors who performed in the vaudeville shows resided during the season at a large house on the corner of Maple Avenue, now Scarborough Road, and Queen Street. Other members of the same show stayed at a boarding house on Balmy Avenue. Luckless neighbours complained constantly about the volume of noise generated until the early hours of the morning at both of those locations. "We know the show must go on," an embittered resident complained, "but must it go on all night?"

By 1907 both Victoria Park and Munro Park had been supplanted by Scarboro Beach Park, which covered the acres south of Queen between Leuty and MacLean. The new park was a glittering fantasy illuminated by hundreds of lights and featuring attractions such as a scenic railway, a room fitted with mirrors that distorted the human body into weird and wonderful shapes, and the Chutes, a devilish contraption that took young men and their dates on a boat-shaped conveyance that inched with agonizing slowness up to the top of a tower before suddenly whooshing down the other side and landing with a mighty splash in the waters below.

Another building housed a re-enactment of the famous 1889 flood in

Some bathers up to their chins in water at Kew Beach in 1908.

12 THE BEACH

The Munro Park trolley cars were always crowded in the summertime.

Johnstown, Pennsylvania. While the audience watched, they listened to the off-stage voice of an actor describing the events that led up to the disaster. Suddenly the lights went out, the actor's voice cried out in horrified tones, "My God, the dam has burst," then the lights went on again and there was the once-thriving little community flattened beyond recognition. In later years, aided by a few deft alterations, the scene became the setting for a re-creation of the 1906 San Francisco earthquake. While the locale had changed, the end result was the same depiction of widespread damage and destruction.

Another popular attraction was called The Tunnel of Love. This consisted of a flotilla of self-propelled canoes that floated along a semi-circular waterway enclosed by a roof. Each boat seated two people and since the ride was conducted in total darkness it was much used by young sweethearts who figured they could indulge in some serious canoodling without anyone being the wiser. However, the boats leaked, so each one was equipped with a bucket for baling purposes. When the craft arrived back at the landing, all the attendants had to do was check the bottom of the boat for the amount of water sloshing around and they would have a clear idea of the type of activity engaged in by the young occupants *en route*.

The amusement parks helped develop public transit routes to the east end. That was approved by the growing population, but historically the waters have never been calm for long in Toronto's Kingdom by the Lake.

In December 1906 the citizenry sprang into outraged action when word got out that the Canadian Pacific Railway and the Canadian Northern Railway were planning to strike a double-edged blow to the very heart of the community. The CPR intended to run a track along a four-block stretch of the waterfront and the CNR planned to lay its track on a route about 200 yards north of Queen

Too cold for swimming, but just the right temperature for watching.

An example of the splendid architecture along the beachfront in the heyday of the amusement parks.

Street. Petitions were circulated, protest meetings were held in overflowing halls, and a delegation appeared before a commission in Ottawa pointing out that if the railway received approval for its plans, property values in the area would plummet and citizens would lose already scarce access to the lake. The citizens carried the day.

Scarboro Beach Amusement Park, with its many attractions, was popular from the day it first opened, but just two years later it outdid itself with what is believed to be the first public exhibition of an airplane flight in Canada.

It was the gosh-darnedest sight the huge crowd had ever seen. The date was

The scenic railway provided a leisurely look at all the park attractions.

American daredevil pilot Charles F. Willard.

September 2, 1909, and squatting in the sand near the Lake Ontario shoreline was that symbol of the future, a machine named the Golden Flyer. The pilot was American daredevil Charles F. Willard, and he intended to introduce the marvel of flight to the assembled throng by taking a short hop over the lake.

His appearance was welcomed by the park's stakeholders because poor weather had kept attendance down that summer, but the committee in charge, without

The amusement park attractions looked even more wondrous at night.

any idea of the special demands involved, had not provided any space for the aircraft to take off and land. The only path the Curtiss biplane could take off from was a narrow alley between two buildings leading out towards the lake. Willard arranged to have a wooden trough placed down the centre of the alley near Scarboro Beach Boulevard that would serve as a track for the front wheel of his machine during takeoff. The buildings between which he had to manoeuvre allowed a scant six feet of room on either side of his wings and the track ended at the top of a three-foot-high breakwater out in the lake.

Under a heavy sky, and with the light fading quickly, Willard settled himself at the controls, revved up the engines, and clattered down his makeshift runway. He was barely airborne when the engine began to sputter. As the horrified crowd looked on, man and machine pancaked into shallow waters about 300 feet from shore, with the front wheel resting on the sand and the tail sticking high out of the water. Willard was fished out, wet, cold, but undaunted. Five days later after completing minor repairs to his biplane, he was ready for another try.

He had better luck on his second attempt. After revving up the engines with a mighty blast that lifted men's hats off their heads and billowed the long dresses of the women in the crowd, he lifted his aircraft off the end of the breakwater at full speed and executed a graceful circle about 200 feet above ground level, covering a total distance of five miles in five minutes. Just imagine, that airplane was going

Canada's harsh winters took their toll on frontages along the waterfront.

a mile a minute! Willard's triumph was short-lived, however, because with his intended landing spot crowded with spectators and his gas tank almost empty, he had but one option. Down into the drink he went again. This time, when rescuers arrived at the scene, he was sitting on a wing of the aircraft, with Lake Ontario's cold waters lapping around his neck. Four days later, with man and machine thoroughly dried out, the pilot tried again, but this time the Golden Flyer's magneto conked out—and Willard and the water met one another for the third time.

In 1931 these homes at the foot of Leuty Avenue were to be razed as part of the development of the new waterfront park.

This proved to be his final attempt because the biplane's propeller was damaged. The aircraft was loaded onto a train and shipped back to the United States. Willard's determined attempts were hardly mentioned in the newspapers of the day, which were filled with accounts of Admiral Peary's discovery of the North Pole, but it is believed that the amusement park air show was the first advertised flying exhibition in Canada.

Willard continued his daredevil lifestyle for several years and eventually died peacefully at the age of 93.

The park and its raffish retinue of jugglers, acrobats, daredevils, trick ponies, and trained cats continued to draw thousands of visitors until the early 1920s. By

A COMMUNITY STIRS

then, the automobiles had become larger, faster, and more dependable, and a network of highways had grown up that could be driven comfortably along. People began to look further afield for their diversions. Attendance began slipping, and on September 12, 1925, the Ferris wheel and all the other gaudy attractions were closed down after 19 seasons.

Six weeks later the land occupied by the park, stretching from Leuty Avenue to Maclean, was purchased by a private company that planned to build a subdivision extending from Hubbard Boulevard south to the lake. However, the city bought almost three acres on the south side of the property for the waterfront park it was planning. The developers began building the subdivision north of Hubbard Boulevard instead and by 1926 were advertising large, comfortable homes for sale priced from $5,400 to $7,500.

The creation of the wonderful park system that is the heart of the Beach was a long, complex process. The three acres the city bought were a building block in the realization of a waterfront vision that had begun in 1912 with a citywide plan developed by the Toronto Harbour Commission. In the eastern Beaches the plan called for marinas, a bathhouse, and a boardwalk, and for protection of the shoreline. It also called for more land purchase and the demolition of existing homes and cottages.

The lakeshore in the 1910s and 1920s was lined with a hodgepodge of tents, cottages, and permanent homes built right to the water's edge. They had to go.

The waterfront at Kippendavie after a storm in 1929.

The City Dairy was founded by Walter Massey of the famous Massey farm implement family. He owned Dentonia, a huge farm located northeast of the Victoria Park subway station.

A 1928 *Toronto Telegram* story said, "Fifty-seven properties were affected by the Controller's decision to take possession and settle later." Prices being asked ranged from $100 a foot at 102 Lake Front to $39,000 for 196 feet at Neville Park Boulevard.

The first major purchase had been Kew Gardens, which the city bought from the Williams family in 1907 for $43,700. In 1879 Joseph Williams had opened the gates to the Canadian Kew Gardens, named after his favourite place in his native England. He called his 20-acre waterfront farm property "a place of Innocent Amusements," where visitors could rent tents or summer cottages and buy fruit and vegetables fresh from the Williams garden. No liquor was allowed on the grounds and, for the first year, no admittance was charged. The next year there was an admission fee but still no liquor. It was a family vacation spot where people enjoyed the fresh air and Williams' "Innocent Amusements" along the waterfront.

A lifelong local resident, Ted Reeve, painted a lively picture of other problems the city faced in putting together its dream park. He became a popular sports writer for the *Toronto Telegram* and was also a gifted athlete who starred in many sports, but is perhaps best known for his exploits on the football field where he was a mainstay on the Balmy Beach club that won the Grey Cup in 1927 and 1930.

Writing in a community newspaper about his days as a venturesome boy of the beach, he recalled a jerry-built structure called the Brushwood Bridge. This was a somewhat unsteady, raised pathway that led across the mosquito-infested Big Swamp in the south end of Kew Gardens, close to the present-day baseball diamond. You had to watch yourself every inch of the way across the bridge,

The placement of groynes played a key role in the establishment of the beach that we know today.

Reeve wrote, because one false step landed you in a waist-deep quagmire alive with tadpoles, frogs and a ravenous insect population.

Eventually all of the marshland was filled in. The houses on the property were either torn down or moved, and only the Kew Williams cottage remains.

Violent storms had played havoc with the shoreline for years. Considerable heat was applied on city officials to do something about it—a battle that would be played over and over again in coming years. In 1929, after several attempts to stabilize the shore proved unsuccessful, the city established a series of what it called experimental groynes along the waterfront, at a cost of $20,000. These were wooden shafts extending several feet into the lake, with pilings at the tip and an arrowhead formation that resembled an animal's snout. The word *groyne* comes from the Latin *grunium* meaning a pig's snout. Typically, there were loud protests to the effect that the groynes were ugly and useless. Calls were made for the Cyclone, a city-owned dredge, to be used instead to restore the sand.

Finally, in March 1930 after the last of the winter ice had left the shoreline, it was agreed that the groynes had done their job. From Woodbine Beach eastward, the sand remained firm and dry, although a small band of doubters maintained that "the first ripsnorting south-easter" would destroy all the advances that had been made over the previous six months. The base of the groynes' tips prevented sand from leaving the shore when the waves subsided and gradually a permanent beach was established.

The final park construction was started in 1930 and was heavily financed by relief work appropriations. Then, on Victoria Day, 1932, amid great fanfare, a new waterfront park, complete with athletic field and boardwalk, was officially opened by Mayor William J. Stewart. The *Mail* newspaper trumpeted: "Dream of Decade Realized with Beaches Park Opening: Vast Throng Swarms into New Ward 8 Areas for Gala Day." An estimated 60,000 people attended out of the city's population of 676,674.

The Boardwalk, stretching from Woodbine Avenue east to the Balmy Beach Club, was an instant success, but not everyone viewed it in a favourable light. To facilitate its construction, the Toronto Harbour Commission had ruled that several dwellings along the shoreline had to be destroyed or removed at the owners' expense. The unhappy residents waged an unsuccessful protest.

24 THE BEACH

Eventually the cottages, many with whimsical names such as Linger Longer, The Merry Widowers, and No Mother to Guidems, were cleared off the land.

A parade launched the Gala. *The Toronto Star* reported, "The parade was preceded by a detachment of twenty members of the Toronto Mounted Police. Then, headed by two postillions in red coats and cockaded hats, came an open landau drawn by six coal black steeds." In it were the mayor and four city controllers. Following behind was an impressive display of local dignitaries, the Irish regiment pipe band, a float carrying the ex-servicemen of the Beaches Legion, and a gaily decorated float titled "The Spirit of the Beaches," featuring "gracefully posed" members of the Norma Griffiths Dancing School.

At the park, the mayor was welcomed with a song by the Balmy Beach School Choir.

Later in the ceremonies, the crowd sang the national anthem while the Union Jack was run up the flagpole, just as the day's bright sunlight began fading to dusk. The program ended close to midnight with an impromptu singsong held around an enormous bonfire. Newspaper accounts at the time hailed the opening as a joyous success, but even after the glorious kickoff, there was contention.

The Parks Commissioner triggered a fight by suggesting that the facility be called Kew Beach Park. This led to a good deal of grumpiness among the Beachers who lived near the waterfront. Residents of the Balmy Beach area felt such a name would result in the loss of their identity. Kew Beachers, on the other hand, felt the proper name should be Kew Beach. In typically Canadian fashion, the dispute was settled by compromise and the sparkling new playground was named Eastern Beaches Park.

Newspapers reported that 60,000 people came to the Beach in May 1932 to celebrate the opening of the new waterfront park.

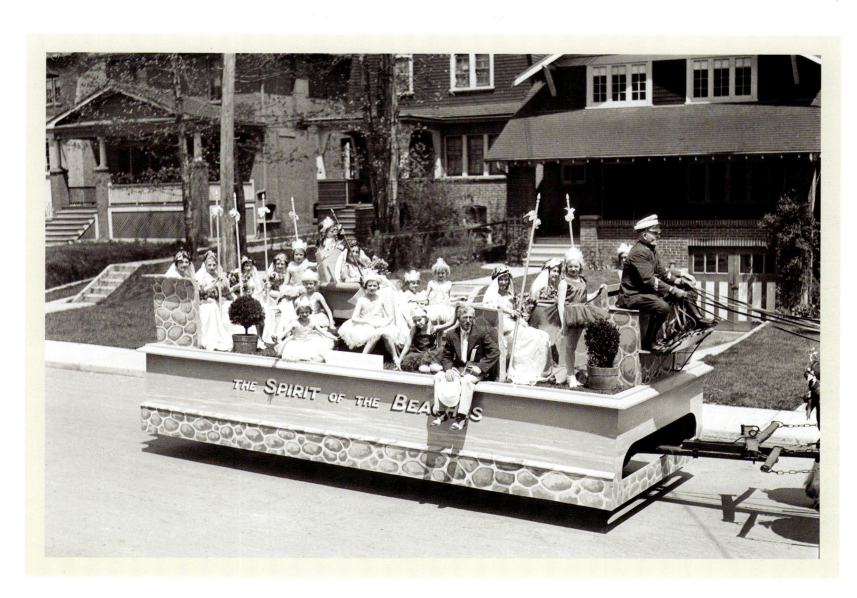

The lovely, young Spirit of the Beach graced her float in the parade that marked the park's opening day.

Visitors from all over Toronto flocked to the park after it opened, but that very success gave rise to a somewhat jingoistic attitude on the part of some Beachers which found expression in the short-lived Swastika Club movement of 1933. These Beachers tended to think the park belonged to them and they were reluctant to share it with outsiders. This is what author and man-of-letters Robert Fulford, a former Beach resident, had to say about the matter some 57 years later: "For a few weeks a number of young men actually walked the Boardwalk wearing Swastika badges but the organized opposition of Jews and the negative publicity quickly destroyed the movement. For their part the members of the clubs claimed not to be anti-Semitic anyway. The swastika was just an old Indian emblem, they insisted, and as for hostility to outsiders, it was based entirely on their tendency to leave orange peels on the sand and their wretched habit of changing clothes in their cars."

CHAPTER 2

Kingston Road

Kingston Road at Dixon in 1922.

Kingston Road at Dundas in 1952.

Kingston Road is a broad-shouldered thoroughfare that for over 200 years has done most of the heavy lifting of traffic into and out of east-end Toronto. Construction on the road began around the turn of the 1800s. By 1816 it had been extended to Montreal.

Stagecoaches were the principal vehicles for moving people and goods overland in those times, but the journeys were not at all like the bouncy, swift travels depicted in Hollywood's Western movies. The road consisted of logs laid crosswise along the roadbed with gravel in between. This kind of road was called a corduroy road because it was ribbed like corduroy cloth. While the hardship that went into its construction can only be imagined, it was just not very practical. The weight of wagon wheels caused the logs to flip up at one end, creating cracks in the surface that shattered stagecoach wheels and crippled horses. By 1831 the road was declared impassable for wheeled vehicles.

Five years later planks were laid on the road from Toronto to the Rouge River, but even with this improvement travellers would be hungry and tired by the time they reached what is now Victoria Park. Inns were erected along the way to provide lodgings for humans and horses. Businesses such as blacksmiths, harness repair shops, and food stores were established.

Then, as the 20th century got underway, two unrelated property developments occurred that had a long-lasting and beneficial impact on the fledgling community. One took place on the east side of Victoria Park Avenue, the second on the west side. The population increase that resulted transformed that part of Kingston Road into the well-established business and residential district that it is today.

In 1896 a wealthy financier named A. E. Ames began acquiring large tracts of land in the Queen Street area. Eventually the north end of his holdings

Kingston Road near Silver Birch in 1922. Horses did all of the heavy work in the old days.

stretched south of Kingston Road from Beech Avenue to Lee Avenue. In 1909, Ames and his father-in-law began subdividing the property, but there were several restrictions placed on the type of development allowed. Apartment buildings were not permitted, and with the exception of the lots on Kingston Road, houses were to be detached, made of bricks, stone, or cement, to cost no less than $5,500, and have 30-foot frontages. In addition, no trees could be cut down and utility poles had to be discreetly placed behind properties.

Newly laid streetcar tracks on Kingston Road looking south between Main and Brookside.

The economic impact created by the newcomers who bought those houses was immediate, but change always comes with a price. Most of the grand, old structures on the Ames estate were taken down as the land was developed, including the Gatekeeper's Lodge on Lee Avenue, which was demolished in 1972 to allow access to the parking area behind the Williamson Road school.

Glen Stewart Ravine in 1934, looking north from Queen Street.

The Ames mansion, called Glen Stewart, still stands on Glen Stewart Crescent, west of Southwood Drive. The spacious interior has been subdivided and over the years a succession of owners has rented the apartments to tenants. But there was a time in summers long past when the mansion was a glittering social gathering-place for the well-to-do and the well-connected in Toronto. When Queen's Plate Week was celebrated at Woodbine Race Track on Queen Street, the governor general of the day and his entourage took up residence at Glen Stewart. Residents used to watch in awe as every day at exactly one o'clock the vice regal party would make its majestic way to the track escorted by the Household Cavalry in all its plumed regalia.

The Glen Stewart name is carried on in another neighbourhood landmark that is, in the truest sense of the word, a hidden delight. The Glen Stewart Ravine meanders south of Kingston Road from Beech Avenue west to Glen Manor Drive. Despite its proximity to busy Kingston Road, it is a world unto itself, shaded by hundreds of old trees, echoing with birdsong, and alive with the music of a little brook that bustles along its length. It was given to the City of Toronto in 1931 by the Provident Investment Company which concluded that the land was unsuitable for development. But the very qualities that discouraged development—dense woods, several underground streams, and steep embankments—have made it a perfect recreational area for generations of Beach residents.

It is also the scene of various rites of passage for young males: the first frog caught with bare hands, and later on, perhaps, the first tentative kiss, and the first taste of beer. Hardly anyone calls it by its formal name, preferring the Nature Trail or, simply, the Naitch.

The word Naitch is not to be found in English language dictionaries, but it is a common one in the vocabularies of Beach residents. It is an affectionate term that conjures up memories of long afternoons exploring bucolic pleasures in a setting far removed from the realities of everyday life.

A short distance away, about a kilometre east of Victoria Park Avenue, stands an institution that is key to the final residential development of Kingston Road—the Hunt. As the Naitch is to trees, so the Hunt is to tycoons. The Hunt was founded in 1843, and from its inception it has been both a playground and a social centre for Toronto's rich and powerful. In its early years, career officers in the British army who had been posted to Canada played a prominent role in the organization.

One of these officers was Lieutenant-Colonel Soame Gambier Jenyns, the last of the Imperial officers to serve as Master of the Hunt. He performed gallantly during the Crimean campaign and was one of the few survivors of the

"The Naitch."

charge of the Light Brigade at Balaclava. As the name implies, the Hunt was formed to pursue foxes, but later other sports were played on the grounds, including tennis and golf.

Nine holes of the 18-hole course were situated north of Kingston Road. As long as that situation existed, residential development was not possible in the area. Then, in 1937, the course was redesigned so that all 18 holes were located south of Kingston Road. The land was opened up to development.

The resultant jump in population led to an increase in the number of businesses established on Kingston Road. One of the people who benefited from the increased commercial activity was a young businessman named Harry Randall. In 1934 Harry and his wife Eva opened a business selling smoking supplies, including a mixture grandly called Randall's Special Fine Cut Cigarette Tobacco. That type of business has come to be frowned upon, but at the time it was considered a step up from the one run by the previous owner, a taciturn man known only as Fred, who operated a bookie joint in the back room. Harry's son Ted eventually took over from his father. Randall's store is still on Kingston Road, though the family has sold its interest in the business.

The Randall family lived above the store in those quieter times. Late one night in the fall of 1939, World War II came to Kingston Road with a thunderous roar that jolted the family out of their beds and broke every window in the building. The Randalls were not hurt. They were not even the targets of the bombing. The fruit and vegetable store right beside them to the east was run by a family named Grimaldi. When Italy joined the Axis, assaults on Italian-run businesses in Toronto were not uncommon.

The Grimaldi family reopened their store, but a much uglier incident occurred at a fruit store on the north side of Queen Street, a few doors west of Hambly Avenue. Simone's Fruit Store had operated successfully at the location since 1920, but shortly after the Grimaldi incident a fire was started in a garage behind the store. The Simone family escaped unharmed, but that was just the beginning. Roving gangs frequently broke the store's front windows and upset displays of produce placed near the front door. Eventually business began to decline. Vince Simone remembers that his father was a friendly and successful businessman who could not understand why this was happening to him. One night the father told his family that in the past the store had always been full of customers, but after the incidents it was always empty. Soon afterwards he closed the store and the family moved away. Neither the Grimaldi nor the Simone case was ever solved.

With the end of the war, the good times returned to Kingston Road. Ted Randall, by then a teenager, remembers a district bustling with action. Duckworth's fish and chips store did a booming business, selling paper cones

Grimaldi's fruit and vegetable store stood at the corner of Kingston Road beside Randall's.

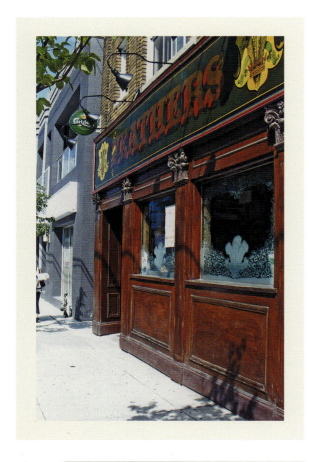

The Feathers Pub on Kingston Road has been a popular local gathering place since the 1980s.

filled to the brim with steaming fries to the area's many Anglo-Saxons. The Laura Secord store sold chocolates that were made in the back. Other businesses included a United Cigar Store and a Stedman's Five and Ten. Tip Top Tailors had an outlet there, and businesses as diverse as Tamblyn's Drugs, Blue Bonnet Bakery, and a Willys-Overland car dealership all flourished in the business district. Thompson's Honeymoon dispensed ice cream cones for three cents. If you could afford to ante up a nickel, you got a double scoop.

Kingston Road had it all, according to Randall. He dismisses the Queen Street business district of the immediate post-war years as just a place filled with junk stores and gas stations. Most of the Kingston Road stores relocated or changed hands as time went on. Willys-Overland went out of business around the end of the 1950s, but Willys will always be remembered as the maker of that iconic symbol of World War II, the famous Jeep.

Kingston Road also had a lively and competitive entertainment component. Movie houses staged audience-attracting events such as lucky draws, and Saturday afternoon film fare always included at least one cartoon and a serial. The Manor Theatre had a kid's program every Saturday afternoon where youthful patrons sat through two feature films and a cartoon, all for the price of 5 cents. Pretty inexpensive babysitting. Another movie-house mainstay operated for many years just two doors west of Randall's. The patriotic owners had wanted to call it the Elizabeth to honour the Queen, but authorities denied them permission on the grounds that there were too many similar requests, so it became the Scarborough Theatre. The Scarborough charged 10 cents admission which was double the going rate, but customers willingly paid up because the seats were more comfortable than the competition's. The theatre was eventually

KINGSTON ROAD 39

The Laura Secord shop at Kingston Road just across the street from the Kingston Road United Church sold chocolates at the front of the store and made them in the back. Forelady Alice Walsh, in the centre, poses with her staff during a lunch break.

In 1929 a streetcar comes out of the loop and makes the turn at Kingston Road and Bingham.

replaced by a restaurant and bar and then eventually the structure was torn down to make way for a condominium residence. Kingston Road's flirtation with the glamorous world of Hollywood was over.

The young men and women of the Kingston Road area have for many years had a winning history in sports of all kinds, but oddly enough that tradition of success did not apply when athletes entered the business world. Back in the 1950s, the building now occupied by the legal firm of Dashwood and Dashwood was the home of a menswear store called Jack Wedley's Argo Shop.

Jack may have been good at running a football, but he didn't have much luck running a business. He gave it up after a determined but losing battle. Before he left, he told Ted Randall that he would often be in his store all day without a single customer passing through his door.

At about the same time, an enormously popular wrestler named Whipper Billy Watson launched a soft drink enterprise called Whipper's Beverages. One day he dropped into Thompson's Honeymoon to promote his product. Whipper gave his drink away free that day, but he found few takers and it quickly disappeared before The Whip was able to put a stranglehold on the market. The beloved athlete returned to the wrestling ring where, given the sport's tradition of somewhat flexible judging standards when it came to local favourites, his chances of success were a good deal more predictable.

Myrt Lamb reached the age of 95 on October 28, 2006. The lifelong east-end resident still clearly remembers a time when the street she grew up on near Kingston Road had cinder sidewalks and the road was surfaced with compacted sand. She and her friends played outdoors all day long and only came home when the five o'clock whistle blew at the nearby Lake Simcoe Ice Company storage facility.

And she remembers when householders purchased cards that were redeemed for milk, butter, or other dairy products, placed them in containers provided by the milk company, and put them by the front door before they went to bed at night. But Myrt (nobody called her Myrtle) also remembers the

Longtime Beach resident and champion runner Myrt Lamb poses with team members before heading off to a race meet in the United States.

roar of a packed crowd at a New York track when she and her three teammates won the 4 x 400-metre relay event at the U.S. Indoor Track Championships in 1934. She remembers the sheer size of New York City and the electric atmosphere around the site of the games, and she remembers being allowed to practise on the rooftop running track of Wannamaker's famous department store in midtown Manhattan. Her teammates were Thelma Norton, Roxie Atkins, and Mildred Fizzell. That's Myrt, second from the right in the team photo. Their triumph was front-page news in Canadian papers, because it marked the first time a Canadian relay team, male or female, had won a U.S. track title.

Winning the race might have been the easiest part of the experience for the four young women. They lacked proper funding for the event, so they bundled themselves into a Buick touring car, threw in $5 each for gas money, and set out for the big event sustained only by a bag of sandwiches and fruit, grabbing sleep in the car when they could. The experience seemed to agree with Myrt, because several months later she and three teammates borrowed another touring car from a friend and drove to Philadelphia, where they placed first in another major race.

Myrt also enjoyed success in local events. When the waterfront was opened amid great fanfare in 1932, foot races were a prominent part of the festivities. A look at a faded newspaper clipping that published the results shows Myrt Lamb winning the Ladies over-18 100-yard dash. She was provincial titleholder in the 200-metre event. When her competitive career ended in 1935, she did a wartime stint with the RCAF Women's Division. When peace came, Myrt joined Ontario Hydro as a research photographer, where she worked until her retirement.

It is gone now, of course, the old building at the southeast corner of Kingston Road and Woodbine Avenue that was for many years the home of the Royal Canadian Legion Branch 42. It was initially headquarters for the Great War Veteran's Association when it was established in 1926 in the former Lavender Hotel. While it was modestly successful as a gathering place for old soldiers, the club's best years began in the late 1940s, when returning Second World War vets added their invigorating presence to the membership.

Gasoline stations were once a familiar sight in the area. This elaborate early model was located at the intersection of Queen Street and Eastern Avenue.

Committees were formed to press Ottawa for increases in the benefits available to war veterans and their families. Ambitious plans were drawn up to improve the facilities of the club itself. But it wasn't all work. The membership consisted for the most part of people who honestly felt they were lucky to be alive—they celebrated accordingly.

Almost every week, the members found a reason to throw a party. The Saturday Night Socials featured Tommy Wilson on the guitar and Frank Ferris on the drums. Valentine Dances, Honours and Awards Day for past executives, picnics at Kew Beach, and Christmas parties—they were all well and enthusiastically attended. And there was the annual Warrior's Day Parade, during the Canadian National Exhibition, at the conclusion of which the entire membership unanimously agreed that the Branch 42 Honour Guard was the best turned-out unit in the whole event. The branch became known,

The Canadian Legion Branch 42 colour guard passes smartly by in the Warrior's Day Parade at the 1993 CNE.

among the membership at least, as the House of Champions, and there is some validity to that claim. Len O'Neill and Len Marshall won many city-wide darts tournaments and the branch has the trophies to prove it. And as there were prizes, so there were personalities, members fondly called, for whatever reason, the Streaker, Stoney, Red the piano player, Turf, and Fish. They are gone now, old age and infirmity having accomplished what enemy fire could not.

In the early days of the Branch, women were not allowed in the club room but they gradually assumed more prominent roles. The Beaches Peaches were well-respected members of the Ladies Auxiliary. Women such as Margaret Foley, Helen Lake, and Cindy Patterson have made significant contributions to the continued existence of Branch 42, which is now combined with the Baron Byng branch on Coxwell Avenue.

Canadian soldiers who served in later conflicts such as the Korean War have always been welcome, but it was the World War II vets who transformed the Branch into a vibrant part of the Beach community. They are almost all gone, but their wives and widows continue to play prominent roles in the organization. Margaret Foley, whose first husband was wounded in overseas action, was the first woman president of Branch 42. She is a distinguished presence, along with male members of the old Branch 42, at the November 11 wreath-laying ceremonies at the Kew Gardens Cenotaph.

But that is the way it is with wars. Old men quarrel, young men die, and over the passage of time their women remain to mourn their loss and honour their memory.

CHAPTER 3

horses and hot tips

Just past the first turn on a slightly sloppy track.

The Lavender Hotel, named after the owner, had stables for the horses owned by overnight guests. These came in handy after the Woodbine Driving and Racing Park began operations in 1875. The racetrack, situated at Woodbine Avenue and Queen Street, was only a few hundred metres south of the hotel, so horsemen found it convenient to stable their steeds at the Lavender.

The 80-acre Woodbine track site was purchased from Joseph Duggan, a prim and conservative man known as the Deacon who had just retired as the owner of Duggan's Saloon at King and Princess streets. Over time the track built a reputation as one of the finest facilities in North America, but its early days were marked by scandal, tragedy, and endless complaints about the poor quality of the racing surface. Owners complained that their horses were in danger of falling because the ground was loose and unstable. The problem was caused by the track's proximity to Lake Ontario, as spring storms inundated the racing surface, but tons of infill eventually resolved the situation.

An accident occurred on Plate Day in 1893 when partially rotted planks on the stairway between the grandstands collapsed and several spectators were injured. Injury claims were immediately filed and eventually the books were closed with the payment of $4,400 in out-of-court settlements.

In time the track condition was remedied to everyone's satisfaction and the people injured in the grandstand collapse were properly compensated but solving the scandal was a different matter entirely. Bookmaking was an ever-present and unsavoury element at the track right from the moment the first race was run in 1875. Bookmakers circulated through the crowds, setting their own odds to fill their pockets while emptying those of bettors who hadn't done their homework.

The Woodbine Race Track back in the days when patrons could park their cars and walk to the popular facility.

To add to the aura of lawlessness, gangs of toughs roamed the crowds brazenly robbing patrons on race days. The jockeys were in on the shenanigans, too. A common practice was "pulling" or reining in the favourite in a race so that a long shot could win at odds most rewarding to those who had rigged the scheme.

Woodbine eventually acquired an air of respectability thanks to the efforts of Thomas Charles Patterson, a lawyer, politician, editor of the *Mail* newspaper, and postmaster. He took command of the operation and launched the Ontario Jockey Club (OJC), vowing to squelch all nefarious practices with a strong hand. Patterson's approach was not surprising since he was known to be a moral man, but his resolve to clean things up may have been strengthened by the fact that he had seen his own mare, Emily, pulled in an 1874 race.

Patterson's tactics soon paid off. The grandstands were repainted, lawless elements were kept in check by vigilant policemen, and the grounds were extensively manicured. In 1876 Woodbine Park scheduled the first of 75 consecutive runnings of the Queen's Plate on the May 24 birthday of its patron, Queen Victoria.

Woodbine patrons show off their finery in a scene captured by Beach artist Donnie Harris.

The final stage in sanitizing the Woodbine operation took a little longer to bring about. The popularity of the track was bringing ever-growing crowds to the facility and with that came increased betting. Governments wanted a share of the swag and it didn't take them long to get it. The federal government introduced anti-gambling amendments to the Criminal Code, which were designed to get rid of the bookies who roamed freely around racetracks. This forced the OJC to bring in a new betting system. The bookies were kicked out of their booths in the betting sheds east of the grandstands and were forced to mingle with the crowds in front of the grandstands. They carried chalkboards on which they printed the odds and were affectionately known as the Knights of the Pencil. The bookies paid a licensing fee of up to $500 to the OJC for the right to ply their trade at the track. They were a colourful lot, each with his own coterie of believers who were convinced their man had the inside goods that would make them all rich by the end of the day.

As it turned out, the big winner was the Ontario government. By 1911 the Knights of the Pencil had all been replaced by electrically operated contraptions called *pari-mutuels*, which is French for mutual wagering. Those who

The betting ring at the Woodbine track was always crowded with racing fans ready to put their money on a sure thing.

backed the winning three horses divided among themselves the total of the stakes placed on the other horses, minus a commission for the operator.

The path leading to the well-groomed status of the existing Woodbine Race Track was not without its hurdles. Early editions of the Queen's Plate were held on a rotating basis at several Ontario tracks, including Woodbine, Guelph, Kingston, Hamilton, and the Danforth. It was a money-making event wherever it was held, with one notable exception. In 1882, when it was staged at the Newmarket Course in London, Ontario, the fledgling Ontario Jockey Club lost

King George VI was the only reigning monarch to attend a running of the King's Plate.

almost $2,000. The executive decided that swift action was needed if Woodbine was going to be a commercial success. They lobbied successfully to have Woodbine made the permanent home of the Queen's Plate. They also used their considerable influence to ensure that members of Queen Victoria's extended family presided over the occasion, since, as the *Mail* newspaper commented, "The Royals are drawing cards." Princess Louise, Queen Victoria's daughter, was guest of honour at the 1876 race. The parade of Royal notables continued over the years with the high point coming in 1939, when King George VI became the first and only reigning monarch to attend the event.

It was called the King's Plate, of course, when King George was on the throne, but after his death in 1952, the crown was passed to his eldest daughter, Elizabeth, and the race became known as the Queen's Plate once again.

The presence of the royal couple at the 1939 race triggered an elaborate series of special arrangements by Ontario Jockey Club officials. Extra washroom facilities were installed in the infield, 70,000 programs were printed, gallons of coffee and thousands of hot dogs were organized to feed an expected attendance of 100,000 track-goers. Scores of soldiers and police were mobilized to cope with the anticipated hordes.

Unfortunately only 25,000 showed up on the big day. The OJC blamed the press, Royal Tour officials, and the police for the low turnout, accusing them of scaring people away from Woodbine with their predictions of overcrowding and tangled traffic conditions. It was not the first time, nor would it be the last, that the traffic situation would play a role in the history of the track.

The publicity generated by the royal visit and continued improvements to the facilities further cemented Woodbine's reputation in the post–World War

The King and Queen arrive at the racetrack amid great fanfare for the 1939 running of the King's Plate.

Toronto's social elite turned out in all their finery for the historic event.

years as the foremost racetrack in Canada, but the winds of change were beginning to blow. Rumours began circulating in the late 1940s that the fabled, old oval was on its last legs.

In 1955 it became official, with the announcement that the track would close after the fall meeting and a track called the New Woodbine would open at Malton. Among the reasons given for the switch were inadequate facilities such as washrooms for stable employees, congested roads, and that familiar complaint that is raised so often in the Beach: "There is no place to park."

The track finally closed in 1993. Bulldozers immediately began flattening the 83-acre site in preparation for the next phase. It was a prime location close to Lake Ontario, near beaches and stores. Bidding was brisk as developers jockeyed for the opportunity to turn the site into a residential complex. It eventually happened, of course, but not before the old track sent a pungent reminder of just what had been taking place there since 1875.

A firm named River Oaks had offered to buy the land for $35 million, but the *Toronto Star* reported on July 28, 1994, that the company cancelled the bid when soil tests revealed that peat moss deposits and horse manure were a potent combination that could generate explosive methane gas.

There are many memories of the beloved old track. Here are a few: Brenda Thibault, restaurant worker: "My sister Wendy got me a job at the Backstretch Café when I was just a kid, 15 or 16 I guess. The Backstretch Café was located between Barns 6 and 7 about where the main entrance is now. I had five sisters and we all worked there at one time or another. I lived on Aldergrove Avenue north of Gerrard Street by Woodbine Avenue. I walked to work every day and I didn't mind that except it was awful cold in the winter if you worked the day shift because that started at 4 a.m. My first day on the job the boss told me I

Polo matches were a popular attraction at Woodbine. That's the fire hall clock tower in the background at Queen and Woodbine.

had to learn everything, cook, wash dishes, and work the cash, and if I didn't learn it all in one week I would be fired. So I learned. I started at $4 an hour and worked my way up to $8.

"Believe it or not, the big seller on that 4 a.m. shift was the roast beef dinner: six ounces of beef, home fries or mashed potatoes and gravy, soup, bread, and vegetables for $4.75.

"Thoroughbreds and trotters raced at the track and you could always tell which type of horse was running by the crowds they attracted. Thoroughbred people were city folks and didn't talk to the waitresses very much, but the trotter people were friendlier and they tipped better. I liked working there but I really wanted to be a legal secretary but whenever I was interviewed I would always be told, 'We're looking for somebody with experience,' and I would say, 'How can I get experience if you won't give me a job?'"

Graeme Moore, horse trainer: "I worked with the thoroughbreds starting as a hot walker and a groom, then eventually became an assistant trainer. I worked seven days a week and lived at the track. Some of the trainers treated the horses well but there were others who didn't. I worked for one trainer who used to beat his horses. They were well-conditioned but he worked them really hard. One horse, a two-year-old, suffered a heart attack and died during a race and it was really hard walking back to the stables with just a bridle and no horse. It was really depressing so I quit and returned to the University of Toronto and earned a forestry degree. I only trained one winner, a horse named Hit Me Again, but I missed the life and I went back to it for a year. It was a cozy place, like a part of the country in the city."

In its early days the Woodbine racetrack imparted a somewhat raffish atmosphere to the area, with its undisciplined army of touts, gamblers, odds-makers, and assorted hangers-on. All this turmoil was just a few blocks east of one of the most elegant and historical estates in Toronto. It was first settled in 1793 by Sarah Ashbridge, who had moved with her two sons and three daughters from Pennsylvania after the death of her husband Jonathan in 1782. There may not have been too many tears shed when Sarah's husband passed away. He appears to have been quarrelsome—records show that in 1761 he charged two of his neighbours with trespassing and later a dispute with another neighbour ended in a lawsuit.

Generations of Ashbridges had farmed in Pennsylvania, but following the death of her husband Sarah decided to start a new life in Upper Canada. Three years after their arrival, Lieutenant Governor John Graves Simcoe awarded the young family a 600-acre land grant extending north from Ashbridge's Bay to the Danforth Road. The first Ashbridge house on the grounds was a spartan structure built from logs cut on the property, but despite that humble start it did not take long for the hard-working family to make its mark in the community.

Records show that Mrs. John Graves Simcoe, wife of Lieutenant Governor Simcoe, visited on one occasion in 1794. In her diary Mrs. Simcoe wrote that her party drove three miles to the settlement below the town. They must have arrived in a tired and dusty state because she noted her pleasure at being served cool water, poured from calabashes. These were gourds growing on a calabash tree on the Ashbridge property that made handy pouring vessels when the tops were trimmed off. It was an unusual tree in the area—calabashes are an evergreen tree normally found in tropical America.

The Ashbridge fortunes were based primarily on farming, but they branched out into other fields as well. In the winter they harvested ice from Ashbridge's Bay and sold it locally. They also established a successful brickworks on their property.

In 1801, John Ashbridge earned some additional income when he was made one of eight pathmasters in the region. Pathmasters were responsible for overseeing the crews of labourers who carved out the roads being pushed through the forests in the burgeoning district of York.

As their fortunes improved so did the family residence. The original log cabin was demolished in 1809 by Jonathan Ashbridge and replaced by a two-storey Georgian house. Then, in 1853–54, the residence at 1444 Queen Street East, formally known as the Jesse Ashbridge house, was constructed from designs by Joseph Sheard, a former mayor of Toronto and a leading architect of the day. Around 1900 a second floor of bedrooms was added. The new addition, with its mansard roof, gives the building the look of understated elegance that it retains to this day.

Five generations of Ashbridges lived continuously in that house. The last two family members to occupy the dwelling were Betty Burton (1907–2002) and her sister Dorothy Shaver Ashbridge Bullen (1905–97). The sisters donated the house and a parcel of land to the Ontario Heritage Foundation in 1972. While Betty Burton moved to other quarters, her sister stayed in the only house she had ever known until her death. Mrs. Bullen was a librarian whose main interests were travel and gardening. The existing gardens near the house are a product of her hobby, but she was not the only Ashbridge to leave her imprint on the estate.

OPPOSITE: *The Ashbridge house at Queen and Connaught. The Ashbridge family was an important part of east Toronto history after matriarch Sarah Ashbridge settled on the site in 1973.*

The Ashbridges were savers. Thousands of everyday items have been preserved for historians to assess, including shopping lists that reflect the price of food and clothing. All of this minutiae accumulated during two centuries of residence in the same house has been preserved because the family just couldn't bear to throw anything away.

Archaeological digs have been conducted on the grounds and they have yielded further evidence of family life, including shards of pottery, bottles, and a tobacco pipe. One item that is perhaps not the most important but certainly the largest in size is an 1888 canoe used by family members that is now on view at the Canadian Canoe Museum in Peterborough. The original Ashbridge family and their descendants occupy a justifiable place in the annals of this community, but there is another community-minded group of men and women whose contributions cannot be omitted from any account of beach history.

CHAPTER 4

the Lion's share

The Toronto Beaches Lions Club has a long history of providing family entertainment in the community.

The Toronto Beaches Lions Club has been in existence since 1935. Perusing the club's minutes is like taking the heartbeat of the community it has served for almost three-quarters of a century. The newly formed TBLC wasted no time making its presence felt at City Hall. Club records show that, in February of that first year, the Lions petitioned authorities for a speedboat to be maintained at the Eastern Beaches, pointing out that the area was becoming increasingly popular with bathers and the nearest rescue vessel was stationed several miles to the west. Nothing came of that proposal, but the club bounced back from the refusal and began a series of initiatives that continue to benefit the community to this day. 1935 was the middle of the Depression, when times were tough and families were jobless and hungry. All during those dark times the club distributed food, and cod liver oil, and even eyeglasses to the needy, thanks to the efforts of an early club executive named George Bosnell, an optometrist who was the first president of the East York Danforth Lions.

In 1939 Canada was at war. The club sponsored its own Air Cadet Squadron and held a fundraiser called Miles of Pennies, in which citizens placed one-cent coins in a continuous line from Woodbine Avenue to Pape Avenue. Although there is no account of the money raised, given the patriotic tenor of the times it is safe to assume that it all went to the war effort.

The money raised in these initiatives went to agencies such as the Canadian Red Cross and the British War Victims Fund. In addition, the Lions and its Ladies Auxiliary collected clothing and blankets that were sent to Britain and Russia.

With the end of the war in 1945, the club's focus shifted to housing and support services for returning war vets and their wounded comrades. It wasn't until the early 1950s that the Beaches Lions turned their energy toward projects of a wider community nature.

In 1953 Mayor Allan Lamport presided over the opening of the children's wading pool at Kew Beach. The timing could not have been more fortuitous. The date was September 2, right in the middle of a 100-degree Fahrenheit heat wave. The final cost of the pool was just over $12,000, of which the Beaches Lions Club had raised $2,159.81 through many community sources such as the club's Ladies Auxiliary, donations from the 80th Boy Scout Troop, a draw for an oil burner (a considerable prize because householders were anxious to make the switch away from dusty, inefficient, coal-burning furnaces), penny banks that were distributed throughout the area, and contributions from the club's service fund.

The sheer volume of the club's activities made it perhaps inevitable that some controversy would be created from time to time. While the pool was being built, the club put up an 8' x 16' sign giving details of the construction. This raised the ire of some Kew Beach residents, who complained that the sign obstructed their view of the park. It took the efforts of the Park Commissioner

The Boardwalk was the original site for the annual Easter Parade. After only a few years the huge crowds drawn to the event necessitated a change to the existing route down Queen Street East from the waterworks.

64 THE BEACH

and the intervention of Mayor Allan Lamport himself to calm the waters and the sign stayed up until construction was completed.

Then in 1963 controversy swirled yet again, of a more titillating nature. For years the club had been running a carnival on the east corner of the racetrack grounds, and eventually the operation was handed over to a private company that gave the Lions a share of the profits. The new operators hired several comely women to stand outside the tents and urge passersby to purchase tickets for the various attractions. This created something of a hubbub.

Some residents objected to what they considered to be the skimpy attire of the ticket-sellers. The press gleefully ran with the story, publishing accounts of the dust-up under lurid headlines such as "Police Look in on Juicy Lucy" and "Claims That Lions Girlie Show Is Lewd."

Morality squad officers were summoned to the scene and after a thorough investigation it was ruled that the attire of the ticket-sellers would not imperil public morals if discreet alterations were made. A compromise was reached and the show went on and some of the costumes stayed off.

Not all of the club's projects engendered such scandalous headlines. In 1966 members organized one of the most endearing traditions in the community, the annual Easter Parade. The early parade route was staged along the Boardwalk. The 1967 event came to a dramatic conclusion when the Easter Bunny landed in a helicopter greeted by long-time area alderman Thomas Wardle and a host of well-wishers.

A few years later the route was switched to its present location along Queen

Clowns, balloons, children, and a dressed-up dog took part in a carnival parade on Queen Street.

OPPOSITE: *Alderman Thomas Wardle was among the greeters when the Easter Bunny arrived in 1967.*

The star of the Christmas tree lighting ceremony surveys the crowd with the master of ceremonies.

Street from Nursewood Avenue to Woodbine Avenue to accommodate the large crowds. Over the years the parade has featured a colourful lineup, including local dignitaries, high-school bands, old cars, young baton twirlers, a modestly clad Lady Godiva, exotic animals including an elephant, as well as household pets and marching bands. Throughout its kaleidoscopic existence the parade has maintained one consistent feature—its small-town feeling.

That homespun aura is also much in evidence at another highlight on the community calendar, the Beaches Lions Club annual Christmas tree lighting ceremony. For many years, families have braved the cold darkness of early December nights to drink hot chocolate, sing Christmas carols, listen to bands play, and await the star of the evening, Santa Claus himself.

For a long time the Santa Claus suit with its flowing white beard and floppy red cap cloaked the burly presence of "Easy Ed" Elliott, a transplanted Newfoundlander and long-serving member of the Beaches Lions Club. He would cheerfully wade through the crowd handing out candies to excited children while making his way to the stage, where he greeted the adoring crowd with a volley of Ho Ho's that could be heard on Kingston Road when the wind was blowing right. Then the countdown began and suddenly the dark sky was illuminated by a dazzling display of multicoloured lights, festooned on what to generations of five-year-olds would surely be the biggest Christmas tree in the world.

The centre of the action takes place around a bandshell named in honour of the late Alex Christie, who had a long involvement in the family-operated Meca Restaurant at Queen Street and Coxwell Avenue. For years the Meca was a gathering place for a colourful crowd of bettors, bookies, and racetrack hangers-on, all of whom were eager to let you in on a sure thing in the fifth.

The Meca restaurant at Queen Street and Coxwell Avenue was a favourite destination for horse race fans.

This information, usually conveyed in a whisper coming from one corner of the tipster's mouth, would be cheerfully shared—in return, of course, for a small consideration. Mr. Christie had no part in such goings-on of that nature, but he was deeply involved in many other aspects of life in the community. He was a long-time member and a former president of the Beaches Lions Club, and a guiding presence in initiatives such as the Lions Club Bingo and the Easter Parade.

The Meca restaurant was owned by Alex Christie and it was a Queen Street fixture for over half a century.

The Alex Christie bandstand is a prominent feature of Kew Gardens, a grassy expanse with an almost mystical grip on the affections of Beach residents. It is where generations of family dogs have mastered the proper techniques of Frisbee catching, a fertile source of nourishment for squirrels and pigeons, an ideal place for a doze on a warm summer's day, and a place where heroes are honoured.

The cenotaph was built in 1953 in memory of the Beach residents who died in action in World Wars I and II and Korea and stands at the northwest tip of the park, a few steps south of Queen Street. There are no names inscribed on the simple monument, but the names and the memories of those forever young soldiers, sailors, and airmen live on in the area's many churches, which traditionally have listed an honour roll of their congregation members who died in battle.

Every November 11, a crowd gathers at the cenotaph for the Remembrance Day ceremonies which are carried out with impeccable military dignity and respect. Every year the crowds attracted to the solemn occasion grow bigger, and every year the number of veterans in attendance dwindles, and that is why we say Lest We Forget.

A monument to another Beach hero stands a few hundred yards to the east of the cenotaph, but the legacy he left the neighbourhood was rooted in life, not death. The magnificent marble fountain, in Italian Renaissance style, is tucked away on a grassy stretch of the park just south of Queen Street and a few steps west of Lee Avenue.

It is placed in a location so unobtrusive that many park visitors may never have seen it. That unobtrusive location is undoubtedly just where Doctor William Young would have preferred it.

The Doctor Young Memorial. The Beach family doctor died treating patients during the 1919 flu epidemic.

The Alex Christie Bandstand wearing a winter coat.

The toboggan run near the Beaches Public Library was a children's favourite.

In 1903 he established a medical practice in a house at 1986 Queen Street East, across from the park. His office was on the ground floor and he lived with his wife and their four daughters in the rooms above.

He quickly established a reputation as a hard-working, compassionate doctor who literally never turned anybody away from his office. Adventurous young men more interested in showing off in front of young ladies than in their own safety were regularly carted from the beach area over to Dr. Young. Injured jockeys from the nearby Woodbine racetrack also frequently required his ministrations. He almost never sent a bill for his services and frustrated

This picture of the beloved library was taken in 1921, five years after it opened.

patients resorted to some unusual payment methods. They set homemade gifts, such as baskets of fruit and vegetables at his front door. During World War I he was given Victory Bonds in lieu of the payment that he seldom asked for. His workload grew even greater when in 1917 an influenza epidemic struck every neighbourhood in Toronto. Dr. Young worked tirelessly to take care of the afflicted—and he was one of the first to die.

Shortly after his death a campaign was started to raise funds for a memorial. The graceful structure that stands in Kew Gardens today was unveiled in August 1920. Dr. Young is buried in the cemetery of St. John's Norway at Kingston Road and Woodbine Avenue.

The Dr. Young memorial is now located a short distance from the Beaches Public Library, but the two landmarks were not always so close to one another. The first public library in the area was a modest facility, located in rented quarters on the ground floor of a three-storey building at the corner of Queen Street and Hambly Avenue. According to contemporary accounts the opening on February 27, 1914, occurred "without formality of any kind." The library was extensively used by the community right from the beginning, but not everyone was happy. In a reference to the search for suitable quarters, a local resident named J. H. Curran wrote indignantly to area politicians, pointing out that "we were to have a dilapidated shack on Spruce Hill renovated for use as a public library but we ask you not to listen to such a proposition. We should have our own library."

Mr. Curran and others of a similar mind got their wish in 1915, when Mayor Tommy Church, wielding a silver trowel, laid the cornerstone for the Beaches Library on the south side of Queen Street just west of Lee Avenue.

That location did not meet with everyone's approval, however. The Parks department raised strenuous objection—they were led by the commissioner, who said the library site was taking up several acres of scarce parkland.

That dispute eventually died down. When the new library opened in 1916, the staff began a series of programs that quickly made it the centre of the community. Small picture exhibits were held in the first year, and Booklover's Evenings began in 1921. In 1924 the Beaches Library Drama League was formed, and five years later plays were being staged monthly before capacity audiences. The Beaches Music Association met once a week at the library and the Beaches Concert Orchestra was started in 1944. Later the focus shifted to poetry readings, singing, and film shows. Amateur play readings replaced the drama league, but through all these changes the library has continued to serve the community's needs. Children's programs are held every Wednesday and the lineup of strollers by the front doors rivals anything seen on the Don Valley Parkway at rush hour.

The library's solid connection to the community it has served so well took another step forward in 2006, when a huge bronze sculpture established a permanent nest right by the library's front doors. The sculpture is of an owl, its gigantic wings spread protectively over five baby owls gathered beneath. It is the work of Toronto sculptor Ludzer Vandermollen. The owl was chosen

Wordsworth the Owl protecting her chicks and guarding the library entrance.

Every Wednesday is Children's Day at the Beaches Library and there is never a place to park.

because of its association with intelligence and also because owls have been seen in the nearby park as recently as 2005.

A contest was held to name the imposing sculpture and the winner was local resident Nicole Brown, who submitted the name Wordsworth. Fittingly enough, her award was a basket of books.

The Kew Williams Cottage on Lee Avenue is a short walk from the Beaches Library through Kew Gardens. Although the two buildings are almost the same age—the cottage was built in 1902, the library in 1915—they are two different symbols of the community. The library has undergone many physical transformations over the years. Its huge expanse of windows, bright airy rooms, and comfortable furniture host an array of services ranging from classic literature to the latest in computer technology.

On the other hand, the Kew Williams Cottage, popularly referred to as the Gardener's Cottage, will, with its welcoming verandah and distinctive tower, forever symbolize the community that was when it was built more than 100 years ago.

It was built by Kew Williams, whose family owned the parkland, as a honeymoon cottage for him and his wife, Bertha Curran. The happy couple hosted many elegant parties there until 1907, when the City of Toronto bought the house and surrounding property, turning the land into the park that exists today. Though many buildings were torn down, the cottage was spared, and a succession of park superintendents and their families lived amid those wonderful surroundings at 30 Lee Avenue for several decades.

The skill of the superintendents and their staff helped turn the area into a year-round facility enjoyed by thousands of visitors. There was a time, however, when the parkland along the waterfront was a place to be avoided, especially after nightfall.

In the late 1970s and the early 1980s, an out of the way area had become a gathering place for dope sellers and their customers. They would meet at a secluded spot just west of the Balmy Beach Club that came to be known locally as Pot Hill.

Things changed for the better in 1981, when a new park superintendent, Len

Stanley, moved into the Gardener's Cottage with his wife Margaret and their son Len Jr. One of his first actions was to enlist the support of senior officers at 55 Division on Coxwell Avenue to get rid of the undesirable element. The police reaction was swift and highly effective. Plainclothes officers regularly patrolled the park. Lands Inspector Don Banks and Superintendent Dave Cowan met every Monday with area businessmen to hear their problems. During the bad years, about 150 arrests were made annually in the waterfront area on a variety of charges such as drunkenness, vandalism, and the setting of fires on the beach, but by 1985 the number of charges had dwindled to a fraction of that.

Don Banks was later made superintendent at 55 Division and he began a practice of splitting up the two-man police patrols in the neighbourhood. "If they're walking the beat together they will be talking about mortgages and the latest movies and stuff like that," he reasoned, "but when they're split up they can concentrate on looking out for suspicious activity." All of those measures worked and within a few months the bad guys were gone, though not without leaving a reminder of their presence. Park workers say that for several months after the situation had been cleared up they were still weeding out the occasional marijuana plant hidden among otherwise innocent flower beds.

The area around the Cottage has been a favourite site for wedding photos, including those of Len Jr. and his bride Irene. The Gardener's Cottage itself has provided shelter for entertainment luminaries such as Jane Fonda, Robert De Niro, Lynn Redgrave, and Anne Murray when they were shooting various projects in the Kew Gardens area.

Len retired in 1995. He was succeeded by Diana Clarke, the first woman to be park superintendent and the last to live in the Gardener's Cottage. When

The Kew Williams cottage on Lee Avenue near the Boardwalk is one of the area's most recognizable landmarks. Thanks to the Parks Department it is almost surrounded by brightly coloured flower beds during the warmer seasons.

Diana resigned in 2005, the Parks and Recreation Department took the opportunity to turn the historic residence into a community facility. Here is where the Rotary Club of the Toronto Beach entered the picture.

Several designers were recruited to assist in the renovation project. Each one created a distinctive room in the Cottage. Donations poured in from both

The Kew Beach Lawn Bowling Club has been in play for over 100 years.

the community and the entire city. When the work was completed, guided tours were held and proceeds were donated to Toronto East General Hospital.

This is not the only local project the Beach Rotary Club has been involved with. Seniors in the community were treated to a movie once a month at the Fox Theatre. The club also supports Pegasus, an organization that helps mentally challenged adults to live a more independent lifestyle and scholarships are awarded to high-performing students at Malvern Collegiate Institute.

CHAPTER 5

love that Leuty!

The Beach is beautiful in the winter also.

The Leuty Lifesaving Station has stood guard on the waterfront since 1920. The boat house behind it was heavily damaged during a lake storm in the early 1950s.

Since it was built in 1932, the Boardwalk on the beach has helped form the identity of this community. Over the years it has weathered many storms, both from nature and from man. The tempests created by man started not long after workmen hammered the last pine plank into place.

Originally the Boardwalk extended east from Coxwell Avenue to a point immediately west of the Balmy Beach Club. Shortly afterwards, some area residents began campaigning for an extension of the structure to its present terminus at Silver Birch Avenue. As usual, dissenting opinions were raised. Some justifiably pointed out that the Balmy Beach Club had brought much honour to the city in general, and the Beach district in particular, with its national and international successes in paddling competitions and the boardwalk extension might hamper the athletes as they went about their training exercises. Another, more delicate objection was raised by those who asked, in the May 1936 edition of a short-lived community newspaper called *The Reporter*, what the effect might be if paddlers wearing little or, at least, unconventional dress had to press through the crowds of passersby on the Boardwalk as they made their way to the water's edge.

Eventually all of these matters were resolved to everyone's satisfaction. The Boardwalk marched eastward to Silver Birch Avenue with no apparent damage

The sandbags were an unsuccessful attempt to halt erosion along the waterfront. This picture was taken in 1929 after a late-winter storm.

This panoramic picture of the beachfront at Balsam Avenue was taken in 1933. Judging by the jam-packed cars in the right foreground there was no parking then either.

to the sensibilities of those strollers who encountered the athletes as they went about their activities.

Right from the start the Boardwalk was an endless source of enjoyment for Beach visitors and residents, but it also provided headaches for those charged with its maintenance. Late winter storms pushed sheets of ice under the Boardwalk and the ensuing pressure splintered large sections of the walkway every spring. In 1952 a storm wiped out the railing that extended some 1,500 feet from the Balmy Beach Club to Hammersmith Avenue. In 1973 another lake storm destroyed a section of the Boardwalk running 1,500 feet west from Waverley Avenue. In those years there were public meetings to demand repair and reconstruction of the battered landmark.

Improved maintenance methods and a drop in the frequency and ferocity of lake storms combined to bring a period of serenity. It ended abruptly in 1995 when a project was introduced to determine if the Boardwalk's wooden planks could be replaced by boards made of recycled wood and plastic. The thinking was that the new material, although more expensive than the original, would be more durable. This tinkering with tradition did not sit well with Beach residents.

The new boards were three inches thick and six inches wide, with a rounded crown. This last element was what caused all the furor. Walkers and joggers complained that the rounded surface was hard on their feet. The most effective and noisiest opposition was raised by the many jogging mothers who lulled their infants to sleep while propelling their strollers along the boulevard. The bumpy surface damages the strollers and jolts our infants awake, they told park officials, before adding the question that really settled the issue against the new boards: "Do you know how long it takes to settle down a baby after it has been suddenly roused from its snooze?" Public opinion solidified around such powerful objections. Plans for the new boards were quietly shelved.

Not far from that experimental stretch of boardwalk stands a building where rescues of stranded sailors and out-of-breath swimmers have been launched for more than three-quarters of a century. While Beach residents affectionately call it the Leuty, its official name is the Leuty Lifesaving Station. It may well be the only life-saving station to be itself saved by the community it has served so faithfully.

The station has been in use every summer since 1920, but years of neglect had taken their toll. In 1993 rumours began circulating that the city was preparing to

A helpful sign points the way for visitors.

Glenn Cochrane, on the left, and Gene Domagala, on the right, help former Toronto mayor David Crombie model a sweatshirt bearing an image of the Leuty Station.

take it down. A rescue operation dubbed Save Our Station, headed by former head lifeguard Chris Layton, and by community activist Gene Domagala, was organized within days. The battle to save the landmark began.

Ward Alderman Tom Jakobek, another former lifeguard, entered the fray, along with a muscular contingent of other past lifeguards, but right from the beginning the salvage effort was a community affair. SOS T-shirts and sweatshirts were sold by the dozen. Harp concerts played to sold-out audiences, in venues ranging from Queen Street coffeehouses and bars to St. John's Norway Anglican Church on Woodbine Avenue. Those endeavours raised a nice sum of money, thanks to the enthusiastic support of the community, but the biggest

LOVE THAT LEUTY! 85

Mission accomplished! Volunteers celebrate the final payment of the Leuty Station mortgage.

A scaled-down version of the Leuty Lifesaving Station, nicknamed the Little Leuty, was raffled off to help pay for the renovation costs of its big brother.

fundraiser turned out to be the hundreds of tickets raffled off for a chance to win a scaled-down replica of the lifesaving station, nicknamed the Little Leuty.

The structure was built and donated by the firm that developed the racetrack lands. It was won by a Beach-area couple with a daughter and a son who were just the right ages to appreciate a spacious playhouse.

Emma and Ethan Tennier-Stuart, the children of Kate Tennier and Hugh Stuart, have long since outgrown the original use of the building. Over the

The boathouse originally stood on the waterfront beside the Leuty Lifesaving Station. It was heavily damaged in a storm and the shell was relocated to its present site south of the bicycle path.

years the Little Leuty has also changed. An artist's loft has been added. It has been used for toy storage, a back door was installed, many coats of fresh paint were applied, and for safety reasons the Lifeguard Tower was removed. But for over 80 years, the original Leuty and the eight-year-old copy which helped pay for its rejuvenation have continued to serve very useful purposes, each in its own way.

The Leuty Lifesaving Station has been meticulously restored, thanks to a concerted community effort. The same cannot be said for every beachfront structure. For many years a boathouse was situated on the waterfront right beside the lifesaving station. The north side, facing the park, had an elegant,

A display of stone sculptures that appear and disappear on the waterfront.

Cape Cod–style façade and the south side featured a huge set of doors opening onto the boat rental and storage area. In summer months, watercraft were rented from the facility. With the onset of colder weather, Beach residents rented space to store their boats for the winter.

In the early 1950s a violent Lake Ontario storm dislodged the building from its foundations. Eventually it was reassembled and moved to its present location just north of the Boardwalk and its old companion, the lifesaving station. The north-facing façade and the huge old doors are long gone, but it still serves as a venue for a variety of community activities, and remains a fine place to duck into while weathering a sudden summer rain fall.

An old sentinel lies on the ground near the Boardwalk. In front of it, a new recruit establishes its roots.

The north side of the Boardwalk, from the Gardener's Cottage to Silver Birch Avenue, is a sylvan area dominated by trees, many of which were planted in 1932, when the waterfront park was opened amid much pomp and ceremony.

Some are memorial trees, planted with funds supplied by family members or friends in memory of a cherished someone who had died. Each of those trees has a plaque affixed near its base, and the inscriptions tell moving stories in just a few heartfelt words. One such inscription honours the memory of Samuel C. Maybin and was placed there by his friend Walter Nixon. The plaque notes that "the beach was Mr. Maybin's favourite location."

There are similar plaques on some of the park benches sprinkled among the trees. One is dedicated to the Bronx Buddha—since there is no further information on the plaque, one is left to wonder who that was and what he or she did to earn the recognition. Another park bench is dedicated to the memory of Larry "Hot Tub" Hayes, a flamboyant Beach resident who raised thousands of dollars for various organizations, including Community Centre 55. His events were marked by lots of noise and attractive women in swimsuits—while all that hoopla raised substantial sums over the years, Hot Tub never took a penny for his efforts.

Another of the plaques is dedicated to the memory of a hero. Ontario Provincial Police Constable Duncan Thomas McAleese was stationed in Simcoe. He got a call one night while he was off duty, from an informant who said he had some important information to pass along.

It was a trap, and it proved to be the last night of the officer's life. When McAleese arrived at the meeting place, he was ambushed and shot nine times by the man who had phoned him. The inscription on his plaque read: "You gave your life. Your family will always love you and remember you."

CHAPTER 6

music man, muscular males, and clean water

The first Balmy Beach Clubhouse. The tennis court in the foreground was destroyed by a winter storm in the early 1950s.

The Beach is generally regarded as a quiet part of town, and that is just the way residents would like to keep it. But over the years it has become very well known for three things, each adding its own unique contribution to the character of the district. The first of the trio is the International Jazz Festival, which is centred in Kew Gardens, just west of Woodbine. The second is the Balmy Beach Club, located more or less at the midpoint of the stretch, and the third is the R. C. Harris Filtration Plant, which sprawls majestically at the eastern end of the area known as the Beach.

In the 1980s a restaurant and bar on Queen Street East called Lido's began offering a few hours of jazz music every Sunday afternoon. The performers gradually developed a loyal and enthusiastic following. Heartened by the success of the laid-back entertainment, owner Lido Chilelli organized a one-day jazz event in 1989 with a strong emphasis on local talent. That marked the beginning of the Beaches Jazz Festival. In 1990 the festival expanded to two days, featuring performers such as the Moe Koffman Quintet, the stylings of Archie Alleyne, a jazz historian and Beach resident, and a popular sextet formed by Bill King, who later became the artistic director of the festival.

Then in 1992 the festival added two evenings to its entertainment plate, the streetfest was born. The increasing popularity of the festival, however, came with a price tag. The huge crowds of revellers which spilled out onto the roadway shared that space with annoyed motorists. The congestion became so great that police sergeant Larry Reeves told the *Toronto Star* that, during the 1996 Jazz Festival, Queen Street basically closed down and traffic had to be blocked off for safety reasons. The following year Queen Street East was closed to motor traffic from Woodbine Avenue to Beech Avenue for the festival. The evolution

from once-a-week party for jazz musicians and jazz lovers to internationally renowned musical event was complete.

Today the Jazz Festival is one mile of music, stretching from Woodbine Avenue east to Beech Avenue and featuring an eclectic mixture of sounds, including Latin, Blues, Cajun, Fusion, Rhythm and Blues, and New Age Jazz—and it's all free.

Local residents have become more or less resigned to the noise and the four-day increase in population. Local organizations such as the Toronto East General Hospital, Pegasus, and the Toronto Beaches Lions Club have benefited as a result of donations from the Jazz Festival. So the waters are calmer now, relatively speaking, but there has always been controversy, as is natural whenever hundreds of thousands of visitors are suddenly crammed into a small space. Many of the disputes have been settled while others may never go away, given the tenacious manner with which this community defends its territory.

Over the years most points of contention have been settled amicably. The capacity of the beer tent has been reduced from 1,300 patrons to 600 and the music ends at 11 o'clock every evening, except for the final day on Sunday when the entire festival puts away the music at 6 p.m.

One question frequently asked is, "Why is it called the Jazz Festival when so little jazz music is played?" Artistic Director Bill King himself answered that in a newspaper interview some time ago. He said jazz guys won't play on the street even though the money is good. They are more comfortable playing in clubs in Toronto, even though they could pick up considerable extra money by selling CDs of their music during the festival. But, King added, jazz musicians just don't think like that.

In 1905 the Balmy Beach Canoe Club opened its doors and ushered in an era perhaps unequalled in Toronto's sporting history. The building was put up in response to a request from a local group called the Beach Success Club that wanted a boathouse and lawn-bowling green. The Beach Success Club was an all-male debating team. While its members earned a solid reputation in their endeavours, it was the Balmy Beach club's athletic successes that drew national and international attention. The Club has a long and triumphant record of success at several Olympics—its achievements are emblazoned on the north wall of the club for passersby to admire.

Women's teams have brought much honour to the Balmy Beach Club over the years.

In the 1924 Paris Olympics, paddler Roy Nurse captured two gold and four silver medals. In the 1936 Berlin Olympics, club representatives Harvey Charters and Warren Saker collected a bronze medal in the 1,000-metre canoe tandem and a silver in the 10,000-metre canoe tandem. Those international competitions were suspended during World War II, but the Balmy Beach Club made its presence felt again during the 1948 London Olympics, when Norm Lane won bronze in the 10,000-metre canoe singles. In the 1952 Helsinki Olympics, Ken Lane and Don Hawgood were on the winners' podium collecting a silver medal in the 10,000-metre canoe tandem. World War II bomber pilot Jim Mossman is also on that wall of fame for his contributions as head coach of the Olympic canoeing team in 1960, '64, '68, and '72.

The club also gained national prominence by winning the Grey Cup in 1927 and again in 1930. The 1927 contest was played at Varsity Stadium before a crowd of 13,504 fans, against a heavily favoured Hamilton Tigers team. Late in the game Balmy Beach was pinned deep in its own zone and, despite the presence of star players such as Yip Foster, Red Moore, Alex Ponton, and Red Storey, it looked like Balmy Beach would be forced to punt, a circumstance that would have provided the Hamilton side with a chance to score and take control of the match. However, on second down, Red Storey fielded a kick in his own end zone, then ripped off a long run that took the beleaguered Beachers well past mid-field—thus inspired, the gallant lads hung on for a 9–6 victory.

Balmy Beach returned to Varsity Stadium in 1930 to face the Regina

Plenty of paddlers needed for this craft.

Roughriders. Once again the Toronto club was a decided underdog. That year extremely foul winter conditions and the tightening noose of the Great Depression limited the turnout to just 5,000 very uncomfortable fans, but they witnessed a see-saw game that was still undecided in the closing minutes. Late in the match, with Balmy Beach hanging on to a slim lead, Regina was pressing and things looked bad for the local heroes. At this point, an injured Ted Reeve hobbled on to the field and promptly blocked a Regina punt. The momentum swung over to Balmy Beach. They ultimately prevailed 11–6.

That blocked punt was far from being Ted Reeve's only claim to fame. The lifelong Beach resident was an all-star in several sports. In 1963 he was inducted into the Canadian Football Hall of Fame. Ted Reeve wrote a popular sports column in the *Toronto Telegram* and his delightful reminiscences of life in the area when he was a boy in the 1920s may be found in the Beaches Library.

A Balmy Beach team digs in for an extra effort during a race in 2000.

Balmy Beach was the last club team to win the Grey Cup. The club dropped out of three-down football when it became too expensive to field teams, but Balmy Beach Club athletes continued their winning ways. Male lawn bowlers have won provincial championships in men's singles and doubles competition and national titles in singles and fours.

The walls of the club bear proud witness to championships won in sports as diverse as volleyball, kayaking, paddling, and ice hockey. The club has been a dominating force in rugby, winning the Ontario Rugby Union McCormick Cup for five consecutive years from 1985 to 1989.

Those are impressive achievements by the men of the club, but the women have matched them step for step, with victories in lawn bowling in the Ontario singles, pairs, and fours categories, and national wins in pairs and singles. In 1995 Glenna Boston and Doreen Creaney won the Canadian championship in ladies doubles lawn bowling. Four years later, in 1999, Doreen Creaney won the Canadian Ladies singles bowling title when she went undefeated in six rounds, playing before a huge crowd at the Balmy Beach Club.

The first structure erected on the club grounds was a marvellous piece of architecture. Its most prominent feature was a grand open porch that afforded excellent waterfront views from the second floor, where club members could easily watch everything that went on along the busy waterfront. On February 7, 1936 around 7:30 p.m., a fire suddenly broke out just as men and women began filing in for the weekly bridge game. There were no injuries, but many trophies were destroyed in the flames, as well as two pool tables and several war canoes. Plans to rebuild began the day after the disaster and the new club opened one year later.

Then, in 1963, also in February, disaster struck again just as people were leaving after a fundraising dance. Fur coats, heavy overcoats, and fashionable hats were left behind as people fled to safety, but once again there were no injuries.

This time, the new building contained features such as change rooms and showers for women. Although women had been prominent in club activities before, the new facilities meant that they could be offered memberships. This was generally regarded as a long-overdue step, although there were some dissenting opinions. One long-time member complained that when it was a men-only club his wife never worried that he was spending time there, but when the rules were changed she always went with him to the club, "just to keep an eye on him."

Many of the sports played by teams representing the Balmy Beach Club were decidedly physical in nature, but there was one competition played in the early 1960s in which the only things that were broken were the rules. The annual BBC Smelt Fishing Derby was staged when the waters of Lake Ontario around the club grounds teemed with smelt, a small fish about the size of a sardine. When the run was at its peak, dozens of club members would gather after nightfall on a rise of land just east of the club and form into two-man teams equipped with fishing nets.

When a shotgun was fired, the teams would thunder into the frigid waters of Lake Ontario and trap the smelt in their nets. The rules were simple: the winner was the team whose haul weighed the most, however, officials quickly noted a puzzling trend once the weigh-ins started. In some cases it appeared that many of the smelts had lead pellets crammed down their tiny throats and others had been rolled in the sand, the object in both cases being to increase the gross weight and win the trophy. Organizers changed the rules the following year and

After the 1936 fire.

The architecture of the original clubhouse had a strong Victorian influence.

decreed that the winner would be the team catching the greatest *number* of smelts, but here again officials spotted certain irregularities. Some of the smelts turned in were frozen, suggesting that they may have come from a supermarket freezer rather than the cold waters of Lake Ontario. This led to arguments and other distractions, which often delayed the award presentations until quite late at night. The annual smelt run dried up completely not long after that, putting an end to the contest and freeing the judges from the moral conundrum of deciding who really had won the derby fair and square.

So what happens when the smelts are gone, the football team is disbanded, and a step or two is lost to the encroachments of time? The answer is found in this paraphrase of an old song: Old Balmy Beach athletes never die, they adapt. They play Oldtimers Hockey and when that loses its allure they return to the same venue where their skill and athleticism were first shaped, back when they were all about the same size as a set of goaltender's pads.

In 1957 a bunch of them got together on the day after Christmas. They donned old clothes and running shoes, retrieved their hockey gear and old tennis balls out of the attic, and started a tradition that continued until 2007. It was called ball hockey and was played initially at the filtration plant, then later moved to the same streets where these men first learned to play when they were kids. They were divided into categories called Big Guys, weighing 190 pounds or more, and Little Guys, weighing less than 190 pounds. The only rule was no bodychecking. The match continued until Chubby, the only player with a set of hockey nets, picked up his gear and left. At this point, both sides retired to the Balmy Beach Club, where prizes were handed out and the combatants sat down to a lavish banquet. The banquet always turned a profit that was donated to Community Centre 55.

Roland Caldwell Harris was one of the most influential municipal servants in the long history of Toronto. He was Commissioner of Public Works from 1912 until 1945—a time when the city experienced a period of rapid growth. R. C. Harris played a powerful role in meeting the demands caused by that growth. In 1914 he was put in charge of bringing Toronto's rickety streetcar system up to date and oversaw its transition from a privately owned corporation to the publicly held Toronto Transit Commission. Under his direction, the Works Department expanded University Avenue southward from Queen Street and widened College, Bloor, St. Clair, and other thoroughfares to deal with the congestion that had become a major problem, particularly in the downtown core.

In 1911 there were fewer than 3,000 registered vehicles in Toronto. By 1928 that figure had ballooned to 93,663, so to accommodate this growth the Public Works department embarked on an ambitious program of building new roads as well as widening and paving hundreds of others. In 1919 there were 407 miles of streets in Toronto. By the end of the Harris years in 1945, that number stood at 576 miles. Harris was also involved in the construction of many of the city's bridges, including the Prince Edward Viaduct, commonly called the Bloor Viaduct.

After organized sports there was always ball hockey.

The rebuilt Balmy Beach Club in 1947.

R. C. Harris was a single-minded person. His impressive accomplishments did not come about without pitched battles with politicians and bureaucrats who questioned his goals, but what is regarded as his greatest triumph may very well have been inspired by a profound personal tragedy. On January 3, 1906, Emerson Harris, the second of three children born to Roland Harris and his wife, Alice, died from a waterborne illness at the age of seven months.

In the early years of the century, Toronto's infrastructure was in a dreadful state. Slums had overflowing outhouses and open sewers, farm animals were kept in backyard stables, and all that fecal matter drained into Lake Ontario, the source of Toronto's drinking water. Demands were made for better sanitation standards. Two of the most influential voices amid the clamour belonged to George Nasmith, a public health expert, and Dr. Charles Hastings, the city's Medical Officer of Health.

In 1910 the city's infant mortality rate was 146 deaths per 1,000 live births. When Harris took over the commissioner's duties two years later, with his son's death still fresh in his memory, he threw his considerable support behind the improved sanitation standards espoused by Nasmith and Hastings. By comparison, in 2004, the latest year for which figures are available, the city's infant mortality rate was 6.6 per 1,000 live births.

In 1913 Harris released a plan for a combined pumping station and water purification plant at Victoria Park, on a 12.8-acre site that had once been home to the amusement park. By 1913, with the park gone, all that remained on the land were a few sheds, a nature school, and a boathouse.

The R. C. Harris Filtration Plant in all its glory in 1988.

Council approved the Harris plan, but it was not until 1923 that Victoria Park was expropriated for $370,000. The usual political wrangling meant that another ten years would pass before actual construction began.

Work on the Victoria Park filtration complex did not start until 1929. Only the west wing of the filtration building was completed initially. A quarter of a century would elapse before the east wing was constructed, and that did not end the criticism of the structure. The interiors, with their brass and marble, were considered by many to be excessively opulent. It quickly earned the nickname Palace of Purification.

There was more to R. C. Harris than his career. After moving to 10 Neville Park Boulevard with his family, he became a member of the Balmy Beach gun club, developed an interest in photography, and taught at a Sunday school at St. Aidan's Anglican Church. One of his former pupils at the Sunday school, the noted artist Doris McCarthy, remembers him as a kind and patient man.

Harris created a legacy of outstanding civic architecture—he also leaves behind an intriguing question. In the 1920s, Adam Beck, the founder of Ontario Hydro, wanted to build a network of electric railways in Toronto as a means of relieving traffic congestion. Harris managed to derail the idea, arguing that Toronto didn't need rapid transit because traffic congestion was not a problem.

One can only wonder: if Beck's plan for a railway system that would whisk people from the downtown core to the suburbs had gone into effect, would today's motorists be enduring the rush-hour chaos that ties Toronto up every morning and every evening?

Roland Caldwell Harris helped create the foundation of Toronto during his days in power, but the Victoria Park filtration complex remains his most significant contribution to the city he served so well. Shortly after his death from a heart attack in 1945, it was renamed the R. C. Harris Water Filtration Plant in his honour. The pastoral grounds of the filtration plant have long been a favourite locale for walkers and dog exercisers, not to mention film crews, but the plant and part of the grounds have now been closed to the public for security reasons since the 9/11 terrorist attack on New York City.

At the same time, Harris's legacy is being extended. The imposing building and its working parts are being restored and brought up to date and a multi-million dollar residue management facility is being put in place beneath the plant. The installation is designed to cut down the amount of residue being pumped back into Lake Ontario and to improve water quality at nearby beaches.

CHAPTER 7

Queen Street

It's autumn in the Beach, and the baskets are bursting with Ontario produce at Suzie's fruit and vegetable store near the northwest corner of Queen Street and Lee Avenue.

Construction of the landmark Queen Street firehall was completed in 1905. The clock tower was added shortly afterwards.

The Beach's strip of Queen Street East begins at Woodbine Avenue on the west and extends eastward past a jumble of activity including bars, restaurants, a much-used library, lovely parks, several old homes, financial institutions, and houses of worship, before ending at the Neville Park streetcar loop. Queen Street is held in affectionate regard by Beach residents. In fact, there was a sense of quiet pride in the community when on June 4, 2002, TVO's *Studio 2* declared it to be the best main street in Ontario.

There are many important structures along its length, and the list begins immediately east of Woodbine Avenue. For more than 100 years, Firehall No. 17 has stood like a protective sentinel on the north side of Queen Street and Herbert Avenue, guarding the community it was built to serve. The station opened in 1906 and the tower was added a few years later. The tower was used to dry hoses, and its clock was an easy way for residents to learn the correct time before household timepieces were commonplace. A city employee wound it by hand once every seven days until it was converted to electricity.

There is a lot of history within the firehall's territory. An important part of that is situated a few blocks south at the Boardwalk and Woodbine Avenue—the Donald Summerville pool. It was named to honour one of the area's most distinguished residents who was a familiar and gregarious presence along Queen Street during his years in office. He was first elected to city council in 1955 as an alderman for the east-end ward, and was voted mayor in 1963. Mr. Summerville had been mayor for just a short time when he died of a heart attack while playing in a charity hockey game at George Bell Arena in west-end Toronto.

A few blocks east of the firehall, a modest commercial building stands on the southeast corner of Kippendavie and Queen with a variety store and living spaces above it. That was the childhood home of the much-honoured movie director Norman Jewison—who could forget *Fiddler On the Roof*? A short distance further east lies a building that is considered to be one of the oldest on Queen Street. The building has been used for many purposes over the years, and it is now a popular restaurant called Whitlock's. Its original owner was a man named Whitelock, and that was the name applied to the building and the various enterprises it housed until somehow the letter E was dropped. It has been Whitlock's ever since.

That discarded letter is not the only thing that has gone missing over the years. In 1989 Gio Rana opened a restaurant on the west side of the building facing Kenilworth Avenue. He called the enterprise "the Nose" and installed a sign in the shape of a nose over the front door. It was an imposing sight measuring four feet high and three feet wide and it enraged nearby residents who claimed, among other things, that walking under the sign made them very nervous. The battle began. Eventually the city claimed that the owner violated by-law 12519, section 35, by "placing a structure, to whit a replica of a nose, which encroaches upon the street allowance," and ruled that the offending proboscis must be taken down. Mr. Rana launched a legal battle but finally moved his business, and the nose, to a location further west on Queen Street. He says he is doing quite nicely, but remains puzzled by the furore he caused, claiming he only created the sign "to poke fun at my own big nose."

On the east side of Kenilworth Avenue, almost directly across the street from the embattled restaurant, stands a building with a much less contentious history. It was called the Kenilworth Avenue Baptist Church when it first opened its doors in 1895. The congregation quickly outgrew its quarters and

"The Nose" was relocated in the 1980s following citizen complaints about the unusual sign.

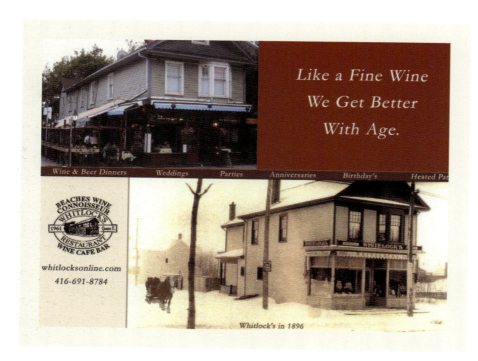

This building at the corner of Kenilworth Avenue and Queen Street was erected in the mid-1880s, and is one of the oldest on the street. It now is the home of Whitlock's Restaurant.

moved to a larger structure in 1908. The first church was empty until 1910 when it was used for a variety of purposes including a warehouse and then a community centre called Kenilworth Hall. By 1920 it had been renamed the Beach Hebrew Institute and has been functioning as a synagogue ever since.

Further east along Queen Street, the wall of the Beaches IGA facing Lee Avenue is decorated with an arresting mural showing various Beach-related activities. It is a fitting location for that work because the Queen and Lee intersection has long been the commercial, emotional, and recreational centre for the community.

Kew Gardens, home of the Beaches Lions tree lighting ceremony, the Beaches International Jazz Festival and countless other local events, is just steps away to the east, as is the Cenotaph honouring Canada's fallen from three wars. Further east, the Doctor William Young Memorial is located on a grassy expanse south of the Beaches library. A bookstore on the southwest corner of Queen and Lee was once a bustling bank serving the community. Right across the street, a local businessman named Gordon Tamblyn opened a drugstore that was the cornerstone of the city-wide chain of Tamblyn stores.

Gradually many of the houses along Queen Street were either demolished or had the first floor converted for commercial purposes. The rest of the house was retained for residential use, and many of these homes are still in evidence, peering out from atop the business fronts.

The Beach Hebrew Institute, also called the Beaches Shul, has been serving the area's Jewish community since 1920.

Further east, where Glen Manor Drive begins winding its way northward, lies a green slash of parkland that was once an urban forest of underbrush and marshland caused by the several streams that flowed through it on their way to Lake Ontario. At its southern end, where passersby can see it as they walk along Queen Street, the parkland is called Ivan Forrest Gardens after the late Beach resident who served as Commissioner of Parks and Recreation from 1964 until he retired in 1983.

In a reminiscence published in the May 1981 issue of the *Ward 9 News*, Beach resident Bob Henderson recalled that in the 1920s and early 1930s there were

two ponds in the ravine. The ponds became much-used playgrounds for neighbourhood children who swam in them during the summer and skated and played hockey on the frozen surfaces during the winter. One pond lay at Glen Manor Drive and Queen Street and, further north, the second pond was created by a dam. Henderson recalled that the dam was another favourite spot for youngsters until a boy fell off it and drowned. He wrote that the public outcry that ensued caused authorities to destroy the structure. Ninety-year-old Beach resident Bob Edmonds remembers the tragedy clearly. He and his parents were visiting a relative's house a few blocks from the scene. He said the event cast a pall over the entire neighbourhood. He believes it happened on May 24th in the late 1920s.

The duck pond and the waterways in these 1924 photos were drained in the 1930s to create the Ivan Forrest and Glen Manor Ravine Parks.

The second store in the Tamblyn drugstore chain was opened at the corner of Queen and Beech Avenue.

The ponds disappeared in the early 1930s, when the streams running through the area were drained into the sewer system. Following that, the Parks Department began the beautification and transformation that turned the area into Glen Stewart Park and Ivan Forrest Gardens.

A few blocks further east, in another of the area's oldest buildings, a popular restaurant and tavern called Quigley's dominates the northwest corner of the Queen Street and Beech Avenue intersection. Directly across Queen Street on the southwest corner is a coffeehouse that started out as the second store in the Tamblyn chain of drugstores, and a reminder of its roots still greets customers as they enter the front door.

Another local landmark stands at the southeast corner of the intersection, right across the street from the site of the former drugstore. Its proper name is the Garden Gate Restaurant but even the most senior Beach residents would be hard pressed to tell you where a restaurant of that name is located. For many years a neon advertising sign hung on the outside of the building with the word "Good" running down its left side. The word "Food" runs across the bottom, so the slogan "Good Food" is proudly proclaimed for all to see. One night the letter *d* in Good was burned out and the restaurant has been called "The Goof" ever since. The dining place was opened in 1952 and even despite extensive renovations it will always be the Goof.

The inside of the Goof before its renovation, left *and the famous sign that has been there all along,* right.

112 THE BEACH

The Fox Theatre on the north side of Queen Street a few doors east of Beech Avenue showed silent films when it first opened in the 1920s. It is still a popular destination for moviegoers. The lobby photo dates from 1947.

The movie-house on the north side of Queen a few doors east of the Beech Avenue corner has also had a name change, although in this case it was more official. When it opened April 14, 1914, it was called the Prince Edward and showed silent films. Now it is called the Fox, and has long since been converted to sound. The Fox is referred to as a "Nabe," or neighbourhood theatre, because nearby residents make up the bulk of its customer base. Over the years

St. Aidan's Anglican Church at the corner of Silver Birch Avenue and Queen Street replaced the temporary tent churches that sheltered the faithful in the 1890s when the Beach area was becoming a popular summertime destination for Toronto holidaymakers.

patrons have endured problems such as a hole in the screen (since repaired), a collapsed roof, and an erratic heating system, but they have never wavered in their loyalty to the 410-seat facility.

By the end of the nineteenth century the Beach was a well-established summer destination. To meet the spiritual needs of the faithful, the Canon H. C. Dixon Tent Church was established at the corner of Balsam Avenue and Queen Street in 1891. By 1895 the congregation was meeting in a pavilion erected at that site and it was immediately popular with summer visitors. The pavilion measured 45 feet by 25 feet, consisting of a roof supported by cedar pillars. Canvas was draped around the structure in case the weather turned bad. It was moved several times until a lot was purchased in 1905 at the corner of Queen Street and Silverbirch Avenue. That marked the start of St. Aidan's Anglican

Church, making it one of the youngest in the area except for Kingston Road United Church, which opened its doors in 1908. St. John's Roman Catholic Church at 794 Kingston Road was built in 1892. Farther down Kingston Road, St. John's Norway Anglican Church on Woodbine Avenue has been in existence since 1850.

On Queen Street east of Woodbine Avenue, Bellefair United Church was built in 1904 on the west corner of Bellefair Avenue. Twelve years before that, in 1892, a small-frame interdenominational church was erected on the west side of Wineva Avenue, a short distance north of Queen Street. As the Beach population continued to expand, it was replaced by a brick church. Later a larger building was needed, and what became Kew Beach United Church was completed in 1914. The two churches, Bellefair and Kew Beach, have merged and have been renamed Beach United Church.

Ambrose Small is not related to the Small family that was one of the early settlers in the area but according to local legend he has a somewhat otherworldly connection to the area. On December 2, 1919, Small, a wealthy tycoon with extensive real estate holdings, deposited a cheque for $1,000 in a Toronto bank, walked out onto the street, and was never seen again. His disappearance, and the intriguing mystery that surrounded it, sparked a police investigation that continued until 1960, when the case was officially declared closed. But interest in the matter never really

Could the Neville Park loop be the final resting place for Ambrose Small, the millionaire Toronto businessman who disappeared in the early 1930s?

ended, and as recently as 1965, Toronto police investigated a possible grave site in Rosedale Valley. Perhaps they were not looking in the right place, and that is when the story becomes Queen Street fable.

The eastern terminus of the 501 Queen streetcar is just west of the R. C. Harris Filtration plant at the Neville Park loop. It is not a quiet ending. The curvature of the tracks is very tight because of space restrictions, and when the streetcars turn, they emit an unearthly shriek that can be heard for blocks. Various methods have been tried to correct the problem, but it persists, and that leads us to the unfortunate Ambrose Small. It is said that those awful sounds are made by Ambrose himself as he begs to be released from the earthly tomb where he has been imprisoned for almost a century.

epilogue

Construction work on the Queen Street line circa 1915.

A storm of protest erupted over the name applied to the area on street signs, and the offending signs quickly came down.

If it is true that, as the old saying goes, it takes a village to raise a child, it is also true that it takes a lot of children to raise a village. That is certainly the case here, where the children of the Beach have been busy raising this community for over a century. That is a lot of years—and it has taken a lot of children and a lot of battles to raise a sleepy backwater into the desirable location that it is today.

It all began in the early 1900s when a railroad company unveiled a plan to run a track east along the beachfront and then north to existing trackage in Scarborough. If the plan had been implemented, it would have destroyed the fledgling community before it got started. The early Beach residents knew this. Money was found to send a deputation to Ottawa where they argued successfully that the proposal should be scuttled.

Sixty years later, just to show that nothing really changes, the city wanted to extend the Gardiner Expressway north to Highway 401 in a sweeping curve from Coxwell Avenue that would have destroyed hundreds of homes and altered forever the heart of a well-established neighbourhood. But the community rose up with a concerted roar, led by the forWARD 9 citizens' association. The plan for the Scarborough Expressway was scrapped.

After the fight with the railroad interests was won—an unlikely result considering the influence of the railroad in that era—the long battle started to change the lakefront from an insect-ridden swamp into the city-wide attraction that it is today. The battles extended well into the '70s, and included the struggle to strengthen the Boardwalk so it wouldn't be destroyed every spring by ice blown in off the water after lake storms.

Up on Queen Street, we demanded an extension of streetcar service from its original terminus at Woodbine Avenue to what is now the Neville Loop.

In the summer of 2005, the TTC roadbed had to be strengthened along the Queen route to accommodate the heavier streetcars.

We fought to preserve our trees and to save our heritage, and we defeated a plan to demolish homes so parking lots could be established close to the waterfront.

We demanded, and obtained, a first-class library and first-class schools.

We saved a Beach symbol, the Leuty Lifesaving Station. When the interior of the landmark Kew Williams cottage in Kew Gardens needed a sprucing up, the Beaches Rotary Club stepped in and turned it into a showpiece.

Through all these years important issues have been well covered by community newspapers such as the *Beach Metro Community News*. The area's history has been carefully chronicled by local authors such as Mary Campbell and Barbara Myrvold.

The Beach as we know it today didn't just happen—it is the result of unrelenting oversight by generations of residents. It is true there is no place to park, but it is a great place to raise children, to stroll along the Boardwalk or in the ravines, enjoy the parks, or shop along the bustling commercial strips, and that is the legacy of Beach residents, past and present.